De-Clutter, De-Stress Your Life

The Step-by-Step, Interactive Guidebook

for a Clutter-free, Less Stressful and

More Fulfilling Life

REVISED EDITION

HELEN D. VOLK

Beyond CLUTTER®

De-Clutter, De-Stress® Your Life

PUBLICATIONS

Albany, New York

Design by Harrington Design, Inc.,
Cambridge, New York
Printed in the United States of America
ISBN 1-930155-08-5

De-Clutter, De-Stress® Your Life

100 White Pine Drive, Albany, NY 12203
Phone: 518.640.9663
www.beyondclutter.com
E-mail: helen@beyondclutter.com

I dedicate this book

to the memory of my mother,

Marion M. Dohrau.

ACKNOWLEDGMENTS

I gratefully acknowledge my students and clients whose support of my work helped create the original edition and this edition.

I also acknowledge the clients, students and friends who since the original version have challenged me to grow along with them.

I again acknowledge the people who read the original version of this book and gave me valuable input: Caroline Wirth, Dr. Rita Madrazo-Peterson, Rev. Joseph Ingraham and Donna Smallin. I also thank the authors Donna Smallin, Harold Taylor and Rev. Joseph Girzone for offering kudos for my use in the published text.

Since the original edition was written, I made changes to the content of my workshops. I also downsized my possessions when I moved from my six-room condominium to a three-room apartment. When my low inventory of books in 2006 called me to reprint the original edition for the fourth time, I decided to re-evaluate the text.

I practice what I teach. Just as I have continued to downsize my possessions, I have downsized the original edition.

A hundred times every day I remind myself that my inner and outer life depend on the labors of other men, living and dead, and that I must exert myself in order to give in the measure as I have received and am still receiving.

Albert Einstein

A WORD TO THE WISE READER

Dear Reader,

I begin this way because I want to establish a direct contact with you.

This book is not only about clutter, it's about **you**. It's about breaking your connection with clutter. It's about reclaiming your time, your energy, your space and your life.

I'm a former clutterer. I live clutter free and offer my transition as a role model. I used the process in this book to de-clutter my life; I use the strategies in this book to prevent me from re-cluttering my life.

De-Clutter, De-Stress Your Life is a practical, self-help book with a positive tone. It focuses on you, the person who possesses and what it takes mentally, emotionally, physically and spiritually to de-clutter your possessions. It's pages are sprinkled with quotes to motivate you, just as they motivated me. I also wove in humor to help you get through some of the fear and stress that accompany change.

I teach De-Clutter, De-Stress® workshops. This book is interactive, just like my workshops. There's space for you, the reader, to interact with the text, just like you'd interact with me if you were my student.

With ***De-Clutter, De-Stress Your Life***, you don't need to choose whether to de-clutter or whether to read a book on de-cluttering – you do both. You actively participate with exercises, checklists and de-cluttering – as you read along. Consider this book your companion throughout the de-clutter process. You not only have my permission to write in this book, you are supposed to write in it. Come prepared with a pen, a pair of sneakers, a timer, lots of trash bags, a recycle bin, a spirit of adventure and a willingness to be a change agent in your life!

If you've had it with how your home/car/office looks, if you are tired of searching for things, this book is for you. Isn't it time **you** de-clutter, de-stress **your** life? Read on!

What matters now, as always,
is not what we can't do:
it is what we can and must do.

Eleanor Roosevelt

TABLE OF CONTENTS

Chapter	Page

CHAPTER 1

Introduction

⟫•⟪

There are costs and risks to a program of action,
but they are far less than
the long range risks and costs of comfortable inaction.

John F. Kennedy

(As quoted in "I'm Lettin' Go . . .But I Ain't Givin' Up!"
© 1998 Tim Riley)

⟫•⟪

OUR CLUTTERED LIVES

We are overwhelmed and stressed out. We've too many things to do and not enough time to do them. Our possessions get in the way, slowing us down even more. We save things thinking we'll need them, then are frustrated trying to find them.

We feel out of control - clutter is all over and we're clueless how to control it. Futility sets in: our space will only get cluttered again, so why bother? Our possessions take more and more of our time, money and energy. Increasingly, we're finding that our homes are filled, but that we are not feeling fulfilled.

We're stuck in our feelings about things, our thoughts about things, our life-style full of things. We're encouraged to acquire things with "buy, buy" messages, and "hold on" messages, such as "you never know" or "maybe it'll be valuable someday." We've been conditioned not only to get, keep and cling onto things, but also to out grow them.

In their book, *Your Money or Your Life*, (© 1992) Joe Dominguez and Vicki Robin point out the conflict between our inner beliefs and our external behavior: that although we spout phrases like "money can't buy happiness" and "the best things in life are free," if we want to be honest with ourselves, we need to look at our behavior which tells a different story – when we think there must be more to life, we buy something.

Clutter has become a part of American life, from the smallest sheet of crumpled paper to the national shame of litter and landfills. On a personal basis, clutter greets us at work, at school, at home and even in our cars. Only a well-rounded approach to letting go of clutter can cut through the barriers to long-term success and take us to a more fulfilling way of life – a life beyond clutter.

There are no hopeless situations:
there are only people who have grown hopeless about them.

Clare Boothe Luce

DE-CLUTTER, ORGANIZE AND SIMPLIFY

To "de-clutter" means to let go of, to get rid of. It's a cleaning out process.

To "organize" means to arrange things so you can find them.

To "simplify" means to make less complex, to un-complicate, to downsize.

Have you ever tried to get rid of a pile of papers by treating it like a deck of cards and "deal" each paper into categories: to read, to file, to the kitchen, etc? What happens? You run out of time so you shuffle everything back into one pile.

Dealing is an organizing task. Organizing before de-cluttering is putting the cart before the horse. It's biting into an orange before peeling it. De-clutter first, then organize.

Downsizing requires an even deeper commitment to letting go: you let go of items you don't use, put in order items you use, then you choose to let go of more items.

"Simple is not usually extreme. Let's do this streamlining... logically, simply, calmly, methodically, reasonably, prudently, rationally..."

Gary S. Aumiller, PhD
Keeping It Simple © 1994

DE-CLUTTERING YOUR LIFE

There's an order to de-cluttering possessions, as there is an order to the grades you attend in school. You start in kindergarten, learn the basics, then proceed through the process until you reach your goal of a high school diploma. You de-clutter your life by starting with the basics, then going through a process until you reach your goal of clutter-free living. De-cluttering is about living. Life is beyond clutter.

After all, you will take none of your possessions with you at the end. Nothing. No thing.

No matter who you are, you only get a little slice of the world.
*Have **you** ever seen a hearse followed by a U-Haul?*

Billy Graham

DO THESE STATEMENTS SOUND LIKE YOU?

- I'm overwhelmed by clutter and frustrated when I can't find things.
  I want to restore control over my space, my time and my life.

- I'm stressed out by the volume of items I handle day after day. It never stops!
  I want less stuff and more time for me.

- I dread having company! I'm embarrassed by the way my home looks and it
  takes too much work to get it ready. I want friends and family in my home.

- I spend time and energy on lots of bits and pieces, here and there. I'm frazzled
  at the end of the day. I want to live more simply, to devote my time to one or
  two satisfying endeavors.

To attain Knowledge, add things every day.
To attain Wisdom, remove things every day.

Lao-tzu

LETTING GO

Conquering clutter begins with a solid process for letting go.

Do you know anyone who threw an item away, yet talks about missing it years
afterward? They have never completely let it go. It's gone physically, but has not left
their emotions or thoughts.

Letting go is not just a physical exercise. It's a freeing experience – mental, emotional
and physical. This book presents a gentle, step-by-step approach to letting go. Its
approach is practical, immediately applicable, yet long lasting. It leads you through a
process so you can attain a more clutter free, less stress-ful life.

If I can change from cluttered to clutter-free using this process, you can, too. Let's
begin.

Accept the challenges so that you may feel the exhilaration of victory.

George S. Patton

4

CHAPTER 2

My Journey Along The Road Less Cluttered

———❖———

As a man begins to live more seriously within,
he begins to live more simply without.

Ralph Waldo Emerson

———❖———

MY JOURNEY

THE CLUTTERED ROAD

I was raised in a house with things everywhere - on the dining room table, the living room sofa, the kitchen counters. If there was a horizontal surface, something was on it!

Mom used to say I didn't get it from anyone strange, so at college, I cluttered a succession of dorm rooms. When I attended law school, my clutter habits came with me. I was married during my second year of law school and continued the cluttered life style to which I had become accustomed, thinking it gave our apartment that "homey" feeling.

After graduation from law school, we bought our first house. Since I was skilled at acquiring but not letting go, the house became cluttered. I was busy and had little inclination to put things away. I told myself I would clean up the clutter "later. I might need these things, someday." I was a busy lawyer, climbing the ladder of success.

We bought a bigger house with four bedrooms and a two-car garage. We moved all of our possessions, including mystery boxes from the attic and unused wedding presents. I acquired new possessions because the house had "empty" space to fill.

In the master bedroom, my walk-in closet was actually a "step-over" closet. Excessive numbers of shoes and purses, unworn clothing and accessories "I had to have" blocked a clear path of entry. I owned at least 20 suits, some of which I never wore, but kept. I filled one side of the closet with dresses, some in protective wrapping because they were

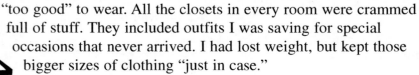

"too good" to wear. All the closets in every room were crammed full of stuff. They included outfits I was saving for special occasions that never arrived. I had lost weight, but kept those bigger sizes of clothing "just in case."

TIME FOR A CHANGE

During my busy law years, just as I had clothes that no longer fit me, I began to examine my style of living that no longer fit me. Life centered on work and possessions left me feeling bored and wondering if there was more to living.

After the death of my father and my divorce, I began a spiritual journey. I explored major Eastern and Western religious traditions. I devoured books by writers from varying backgrounds and beliefs about spirituality. One day, while sitting on the front steps of a holistic health center which overlooked a lake and mountains, I realized that no major religious belief system taught that personal security or happiness came from material possessions. I remember hearing in my mind: "No religion teaches that the purpose of life is the hoarding of stuff."

I didn't realize then how that thought would influence me. It set my life on a new path.

THE ROAD LESS CLUTTERED

I decided to let go of the clutter in my space and downsize my living style. I sold the big four-bedroom house – less space meant less room to clutter. Selling the house was the easy part; emptying it was the hard part. I had ten rooms, an attic, basement and two-car garage to empty! Through that experience I learned how to let go -- without regret.

I was inspired by Mahatma Gandhi who gained contentment and freedom from letting go. Jesus taught not to center life on material things.

While looking for a condominium which would meet my long-term needs, I moved into a spacious one-bedroom apartment with a den and a large storage area in the basement. I'd gotten rid of a lot of possessions, but the apartment, the storage area and closets were full of things. Over time, I continued letting go of furniture, clothing and other items. A few years later, I was able to move into a one-bedroom apartment without a den.

In August 1983, I bought a two-bedroom condominium. It had no garage, no basement and no floor space in the attic. All my possessions fit comfortably in my living space.

During these years, I continued my spiritual journey. Having downsized possessions, I began unraveling other levels of clutter – commitments, debt and "to do" lists. I was a successful attorney with a secure job, had created the local chapter of the women's bar association and was the first woman attorney to achieve certain positions. I was busy, inflexible, always in charge and worked long hours.

I began to lose interest in climbing the ladder of success. When it came time to take the presidency of the local women's bar chapter, I turned it down. I was into letting go, not acquiring.

DEATH OF MY MOTHER

In 1989, my path toward a more simple life accelerated after my mother died. I took less from her estate than I was entitled to and left the estate details to my brother. Mom had downsized her life years before, keeping only the essentials. She became my model for living simply.

I started a new round of de-cluttering possessions. I emptied an upstairs hall closet and converted it into a library. I selected books to fit in my limited library space, then donated all the books that remained on my wall-to-wall bookcases. I sold the bookcases. Also, I emptied the cabinets in my kitchen so I could have them replaced and let go of a lot of kitchen items, rather than put them back in the new cabinets.

My Mom's death led me to acknowledge that I no longer liked the work I was doing. A month after Mom died I caught myself saying to a friend at work, "Who knows? Maybe I'll just quit and go south for the winter." Five months later I stepped out in faith. Without a job to replace it, I quit the job I could have had for the rest of my life, got in my car and traveled south for the winter. I went from being an overly-structured lawyer surrounded by things and people, to an unstructured, unemployed person with a solitary existence.

I think of my trip south as my wilderness experience. During the long drive home, I had time to reflect. Letting go transformed my life. De-cluttering things was a necessary preliminary step to letting go on other levels. If I hadn't de-cluttered possessions first, I couldn't have left law. I would have been trapped by an excessive style of living that needed substantial financial support.

I also realized during my drive home that if I could live for months without the condo full of stuff, I didn't *need* those things. Once home, I de-cluttered my possessions again, making more space for further change.

LIFE BEYOND CLUTTER

What would I do for a living? A few months after I had come home, a friend suggested I make my life work teaching others to unclutter their lives. My heart leapt at the idea. I founded Beyond Clutter in May 1991, offering de-clutter workshops through adult education programs. Students responded with requests for help. Articles appeared in local newspapers featuring the "Clutter buster." Requests for help followed. I appeared on television and was designated by a local radio personality as "the De-Clutter Queen." Beyond Clutter seemed to have a life of its own.

I needed to set up a home office. I moved my few dining room pieces into the end of my L-shaped living room and set up a home office in the dining room.

After a few years with this fast-growing business, I made space in my schedule to write. I published three booklets and outgrew my small home office. I sold the bedroom furniture in my large upstairs guest room and reclaimed that large room for my office. (I also reclaimed my dining room!) I finished the original edition of this book.

I wrote two more booklets and another book, **_Beyond Office Clutter_**. I continued offering workshops, giving talks and working with clients, regularly re-motivating myself to let go. Over time, the condo became too big for me. I had created all the space I needed upstairs by adding to the office a small refrigerator, a microwave oven and coffee pot. Except for special occasions, I rarely used the living room and dining area. I went downstairs only when I wanted to go outside. In 2004, I sold the condo and moved into a newly-built apartment complex. I downsized from six rooms to three.

This revised edition is a result of this last downsizing. I've now de-cluttered my de-clutter book.

Throughout this time, I wanted my home to be my _sanctum sanctorum_. My home changed as I changed, but **the bottom line** has been my spiritual need to want to come home, to **be** home down to the core of my being.

Underneath all the clutter, I have found joy.

At the beginning of my journey along the road less cluttered, the following excerpt from *The Dragon Doesn't Live Here Anymore* inspired me to create my home as my *sanctum sanctorum*. I read it during my workshops and talks to motivate attendees to de-clutter their lives. May it motivate you, too.

We can use the routine experiences in our lives to practice the power of decision and precision. Arriving at the meeting on time, keeping our car in good condition, and carrying out an errand that we promised someone are good ways to mobilize decisive strength. The time of the meeting, the health of the car, and the nature of the errand are not nearly as important as our ability to make a commitment and stick to it. If we master little decisions, the big ones will come easy.

I will share with you a very powerful method that I have discovered for keeping my whole life in order: I keep my room clean. Our rooms are pictures of our consciousness. If you want to clean up your consciousness, then clean up your room. See if you have any cobwebs or "dustbunnies." If so, you have allowed indecision and inertia to creep into your temple. A very efficient and successful man I know said that the little balls of dust that accumulate in the corners of uncared-for-rooms are manifestations of unconsciousness. I believe it. Sweep them away, and in so doing you sweep away your unconsciousness.

When a room is tidy and orderly, a vibration of power and harmony builds up in it, one which blesses everyone who walks into the room, by its reflection of Godly order…We have the ability… to make our homes and our rooms our sanctum sanctorum – a holy refuge. Such order is a tremendous support to our spiritual work. I can remember times when I walked into my house with the affairs of the day on my shoulders. The moment I walked into a clean room, I felt my troubles lifted off of me, as if gentle angel winds brushed off my shoulders. This blessing was not a result of chance, but *decision*. (pages 295-296)

© 1981 Alan Cohen
The Dragon Doesn't Live Here Anymore

CHAPTER 3

Your History with Clutter

"Often people attempt to live their lives backwards:
they try to have more things, or more money,
in order to do more of what they want so they will be happier.
The way it actually works is the reverse.
You must first be who you really are, then do what you need to do,
in order to have what you want."

Margaret Young, quoted in *The Artist's Way*

READER'S EXERCISE

Reader, reflect on **your** connection with possessions.
Use brief phrases, not full sentences.

1. List key points (memories) of your parents relationship with possessions.

A. Mom

_____

_____

_____

B. Dad

_____

_____

_____

2. What memories do you have of your childhood with things?

_____

_____

_____

3. What childhood messages did you learn about possessions?
(For example: to keep things "just in case" or, it's okay to throw your clothes on the floor)

_____

_____

_____

4. What led you to buy this book?

_____

_____

_____

As adults, we need to replace some of the messages we learned as children with more productive messages. Children easily can confuse possessions with love. As adults, we may acquire possessions as symbols of love, but if our early needs of love were not met, no amount of things will compensate.

We often use people or events in our past to find reasons for our shortcomings. But it does not move us forward to blame forces outside of ourselves for our clutter.

No scapegoats!   No excuses!   No blame!

THE BOTTOM LINE?

It's *your* clutter. *You* are responsible for it.

Each of us is responsible for the clutter in our lives. You are responsible for your clutter. I am responsible for mine. We are responsible for our society's clutter.

All clutter is self-created by something we (1) do (throwing your coat over the chair, rather than hanging it in the closet) or (2) don't do (when you order from a catalog, you do not check a box that says you don't want your name shared).

Things don't come into our lives on their own. You or I bring them in or you or I allow them in. I created my clutter. You created your clutter.

THE GOOD NEWS:

By starting from this responsible position, you can take purposeful action to change from a cluttered life, to clutter-free living. Yes, you can!

There's only one corner of the universe you can be certain of improving and that's your own self.

Aldous Huxley

WHERE ARE YOU NOW?

✔ **Check all the boxes that apply to you.**

❏ My life is surrounded by things, too many things. My clutter seems to have taken over. I need to learn how to let go.

❏ I brought things into my life to enhance my life, but clutter has become my focus of living. I want to let go of "stuff" and take back my life.

❏ I think my things **are** my memories and if I let them go, I'll lose my memories. Yet, I can't find precious items buried in the mounds of clutter.

❏ I handle things over and over again. I want to let go of the habits that increase clutter's overwhelmingness.

❏ I have created a mess in my house, my car, my office, even my mind. I want to reduce the chaos in my life and find peace. I want to change from a cluttered to a clutter-free way of living.

Add two of your current clutter conditions and what you want:

❏ _____

❏ _____

As long as a man stands in his own way,
everything seems to be in his way.

Ralph Waldo Emerson

HEADLINE EXERCISE

Pretend you are writing a personal "headline" of your current cluttered life and a sub-headline of what you want to achieve. Remember, a headline is a BIG, bold heading at the beginning. It condenses the content into a few key words.

Example? Here's my headline:

VOLK
SURROUNDED BY THINGS,
FREES HERSELF

Write your personal headline here:

_____

_____

_____

The battle is not to the strong alone;
it is to the vigilant, the active, the brave.

Patrick Henry

CHAPTER 4

Clutter and the Price
You Pay For It

Just as a picture is drawn by an artist,
surroundings are created
by the activities of the mind.

Buddha

IS THIS YOU?

You navigate the room by walking between overflowing stacks of magazines, such as *National Geographic, Woman's Day* and *Popular Mechanics* collected over the last ten years but never read. Several months of daily newspapers lean haphazardly next to these magazine mounds. Together, they look as if they form a wall.

Nearby, file boxes filled to the brim with papers and documents seem ready to burst their seams. Uncared-for books lay in a vertical heap that goes from floor to ceiling. They were going to be read someday but were replaced by newer ones that also lay unread.

Are you in the archives of a library or a research center? No! You're in the basement of a home owned by a cluttered person, someone who acquires but doesn't let go.

You can't wait to get out of this cluttered environment, to leave the mess behind.

Wanting to leave, you look to the top of the stairs and size up the hurdle posed by clutter on each step – years of scrapbook treasures and photographs not yet in albums, old Christmas cards received and waiting to be sorted, new greeting cards thought lost and therefore, never sent. They've deteriorated so they aren't good enough to send out, but they're "too good" to throw out.

For the sake of your sanity, you quickly climb the stairs and get out of the basement.

"Phew!" you exclaim as you close the door behind you, glad to escape the overwhelming amount of clutter.

Is this you?

We are constantly faced by great opportunities brilliantly disguised as insoluble problems.

Lee Iococca

CHARACTERISTICS OF CLUTTER

You can't get rid of clutter unless you can recognize it. How can you tell clutter from items which do not clutter your life? What does clutter look like?

What does clutter look like?

- Clutter is in your way. It's the stuff you move out of the way to find what you want, like that flyer announcing a new de-cluttering book - it's in the pile somewhere. Every paper you pass by on the way to finding the one you're looking for, clutters your life.

- Clutter is usually obvious. It's heaped or piled on the dining room table, kitchen counters, bedroom floor, or oozes out of drawers, bags or cabinets. It's out in the open for everyone to see.

- Clutter may be sneaky. You bring it in because "it's free" (pens, travel information, etc.) or through your "more is better" thinking (if one is good, three must be better and six are better yet!)

- Clutter is an excess number of things -- more than you use or could ever use. (fourteen measuring cups? fifty pair of shoes?)

- Clutter is the physical evidence of postponed decision making. Your excuses, your hold-on thoughts cause clutter to stay and grow.

- Clutter is the end product of cluttered thinking and your emotional attachment to inanimate objects.

- Clutter, when in view, causes a negative reaction. When you see clutter, you have a "kick in the gut" feeling. "Oh, No! What a mess."

Not everything that counts can be counted.
Not everything that can be counted counts.

Albert Einstein

READER'S EXERCISE

A. What clutters your life?

Jot here three similarities in your life to "Is This You?" Examples: you have clutter lining the cellar steps, your photos aren't in albums.

1._____

2._____

3._____

B. Based on the characteristics of clutter, what clutters your life?

List items you have that fit each category:

1. **I move out of the way**_____

2. **My obvious clutter includes** _____

3. **My sneaky clutter includes** _____

4. **I have excess numbers of** _____

5. **I put off getting rid of** _____

6. **I am emotionally attached to** _____

7. **I react physically to** _____

Before you set up procedure which will keep you organized,
you have to clean up the mess.

Harold Taylor
Making Time Work For You (1998)

THE PRICE OF CLUTTER

Situation #1

Have you ever been in the middle of a project and not been able to find an ingredient or tool you needed? To complete what you started, did you get into the car, leave everything in progress, drive to the store for one item, pay full price, then drive back home? Did you purchase a few more items while you were out?

The Price of Clutter = wasted time, wasted money, wasted energy, a delayed project.

Situation #2

Your favorite Aunt Bessie calls you from the Thruway unexpectantly and excitedly says, "Surprise! I'll be there in 15 minutes." Then she hangs up the phone. At first, you are excited, but you become anxious at the prospect of a guest! "Oh, no!"

Would you be embarrassed if Aunt Bessie saw the way you live?

Do you frantically "pick up" the house? Do you hide things — shove stuff into boxes, closets, the basement or under the bed?

The Price of Clutter? Stress, embarrassment, energy and time spent on clutter.

The price of clutter is not only the money originally spent on things. The price you pay begins there. Complete the checklists to discover the stress clutter creates in your life.

Money and possessions are like diet soda –
they satisfy momentarily, but they do not nourish.

Kevin Anderson
Divinity in Disguise

Checklist
✔ Check each price you pay for clutter in your life:

EMOTIONAL STRESS

❑ Clutter weighs me down, is a burden to me.

❑ I worry about breakage, loss, theft, fire, repairs and/or insurance premiums.

❑ I feel embarrassed.

❑ I feel tired, discouraged and/or overwhelmed by my clutter.

❑ I'm overwhelmed and don't appreciate my things like I used to.

❑ I berate myself for being out of control, messy.

MENTAL STRESS

❑ I can't remember where I put things.

❑ I need to figure out how to organize things: alphabetize, sort, categorize, file.

❑ I can't think straight around clutter.

❑ I dread trying to find the "perfect" gift.

LOST TIME

❑ I waste time looking for things.

❑ Clutter creates work for me and work takes time from other activities.

❑ I spend time to pick things up, put things back, store things.

❑ I spend time to take things up to the attic, bring them down from the attic, take them down to the basement, bring them up from the basement.

❑ I spend time to repair, protect and clean things -- wash, dry, air, dust, polish, scour, paint, stain, remove stains, etc.

❑ Clutter creates errands for me - repair, clean, return, send things. Errands take time and gasoline and are stressful.

MONEY WASTED

❑ It's easier for me to buy a new item rather than search for one I already have.

❑ I spend money to replace items I've lost from carelessness or laziness.

❑ I spend money to repair or replace broken, bent, damp, smelly, spotted, rusted, dented, frayed, unglued, torn or otherwise damaged items.

❑ Rather than invite people to eat at my cluttered home, I take them out to eat.

❑ I house guests in motels, rather than at my cluttered home.

❑ I spend my assets on things I don't use rather than save or invest my money.

❑ I incur debt for things that become wasted from spoilage, outdated or incomplete, like missing puzzle pieces, missing parts of all kinds.

SAFETY HAZARDS

❑ Clutter causes fire hazards – I have excess paper and plastic.

❑ Stuff on the stairs, stuff in hallways, stuff on the floor next to the desk, stuff beside my bed may cause me or someone else to trip and fall.

❑ My clutter may cause environmental illness from dust, mold, mildew.

❑ Outdated medicines, hazardous chemicals pose ingestion hazards.

❑ Misplaced records, documents or cash causes me financial stress.

JOB STRESS

❑ Clutter reduces my productivity, effectiveness.

❑ I feel overwhelmed, out of control at the office.

❑ I have disagreements with co-workers/boss over my messy work space.

❑ I am embarrassed about my work space appearance.

❑ I have a reputation/perception as being disorganized, not professional.

RELATIONSHIP STRESS

❏ I have disagreements with my spouse/children/ parents about my clutter.

❏ Clutter increases the effort it takes me to get ready for guests/parties.

❏ I accept and keep useless gifts rather than ask for what I want.

❏ Choosing gifts adds stress to celebrations, such as birthdays or anniversaries.

❏ The quantity of things we exchange at Christmas detracts from the meaning of the holiday for me.

SUMMARY

The total number of boxes is 38. Your total is _____ .

Are you more aware of the price you pay for clutter?   ❏ Yes   ❏ No

---

Helen's Hint:
Whenever you think you don't have time to de-clutter
or that de-cluttering isn't important enough,
read aloud your checked boxes.

---

*The only real voyage of discovery
consists not in seeking new landscapes,
but in having new eyes.*

Marcel Proust

UPPING THE ANTE

Feel more stressed? It may be because you now are aware of all the stressful effects of your clutter. Awareness is an important part of the process. Why is it important?

Two Reasons:

1. People act to either avoid pain or gain pleasure. By unmasking the pain of clutter you increase your motivation to change so you can avoid the pain.

2. Advertisers' constant messages present only the positive side of buying and owning things. In reality, there are both pros and cons. You've unmasked the negatives of owning things so you are able to balance the media's pro messages with the cons.

Consider this:

In her novel, *A Patchwork Planet*, (©1998) Anne Tyler features a company "Rent-A-Back" which does odd jobs for people. The main character, while cleaning out a house of a client who has died, says:

> **"Every now and then, in this job, I suddenly understood that you really, truly can't take it with you. I don't think I ordinarily grasped the full implications of that. Just look at all the possessions a dead person leaves behind: every last one, even the most treasured. No luggage is permitted, no carry-on items, not a purse, not a pair of glasses. You spend seven or eight decades acquiring your objects, arranging them, dusting them, insuring them; then you walk out with nothing at all, as bare as the day you arrived."** (pages. 284-5)

CHAPTER 5

The Thoughts (Self-Talk) That Keep You Stuck

———➤-0-◄———

All that is
is the result of what we have thought.

Buddha

———➤-0-◄———

INTRODUCTION

When a clutter thought enters your mind, you fill space in the physical world with a "thing." First the thought, then the thing. For example, if you think "Maybe I'll use this someday," you will keep the item. The thing and the thought both remain.

We talk to ourselves all the time. It's self-talk – the statements we repeat to ourselves in our heads. These statements influence our motivation and our actions. When we face an item we want to de-clutter, we have a thought about it. That thought may be quick, offering just one reason to hold on to the item. Or, it may be a running dialogue about our shortcomings, with thought after thought listing reasons why we can't let it go. Ah, the mental clutter we have in our heads!

It's time you hear what you say to yourself so you can unmask the thoughts that keep you stuck in clutter.

✎ READER'S EXERCISE

Check all the statements *you* say to *yourself*. Edit them to fit into your language.

❏ Maybe I'll need it someday.

❏ Maybe I'll read it someday.

❏ Maybe I'll wear it again someday.

❏ Maybe it'll be valuable someday.

❏ It's too good to throw out.

❏ I spent good money on it.

❏ It was a gift.

❏ It was my mother's.

❏ It was my grandfather's.

❏ I'll do it later.

❏ I'll do it tomorrow.

❏ I'll do it when the kids leave home.

❏ I'll do it when I retire.

❏ I'll do it when the kids come home.

❏ I don't have time to deal with clutter.

❏ I have more important things to do.

❏ There are other things I'd rather do.

❏ I won't start unless I can finish.

❏ I have to wait until I find 4-5 hours.

❏ I don't know where to start.

❏ I can't throw anything away.

❏ I tried to de-clutter – it doesn't work.

❏ There's nothing I can do about it.

❏ I don't want to make a mistake.

❏ I have to find someone who can use it.

❏ I'm so far behind, I'll never catch up. Why bother?

❏ I've saved it, so it must be important.

❏ It's still good.

❏ It was a bargain.

❏ I don't want to waste it.

❏ I can always use a bag/pin/box, etc.

❏ It has sentimental value.

Other phrases?

❏ _____

❏ _____

Total the number of checkmarks including phrases you added. Total # _____

List here the three clutter thoughts you say to yourself <u>most often</u>.

1. _____

2. _____

3. _____

Say these three thoughts aloud. Are they discouraging?   ❏ Yes   ❏ No

Do they inspire you to act?   ❏ Yes   ❏ No

Do you see how these thoughts keep you stuck in clutter?   ❏ Yes   ❏ No

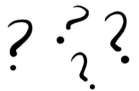

Conclusions

- Negative self-talk leads to stress, drained energy, indecision, inaction and feelings of powerlessness. It enables your cluttered lifestyle to continue.

- Negative thoughts damage your confidence. Unknowingly, you magnify the de-cluttering task and discourage yourself from tackling it.

- Negative thoughts lead you to procrastinate or give up. You stay stuck.

- With repetition, negative thoughts become self-fulfilling. They produce a spiral of negativity that keeps lowering your capacity and willingness to de-clutter.

- Negativity blinds you to what you can do.

You create your clutter – it starts with the clutter in your head.

The ancestor to every action is a thought.

Ralph Waldo Emerson

Example

Let's examine the thoughts and behavior of a person who clutters and see how changing the thoughts change his/her behavior.

Imagine sitting in a public place with one of those stanchions of travel literature. You watch someone select one travel brochure, then another and yet another. What thoughts create brochure clutter?

"Maybe I'll (we'll) go there, someday." and "They're free!"

Let's see what the person could say to his/herself to change his/her thinking from clutter thoughts to clutter prevention thoughts so s/he leaves the brochures there, rather than take them home.

1. Maybe I'll (we'll) go there, someday.

"Then again, maybe we won't. I was bored. These places look interesting, but I'm not in the market for travel information right now. When I want to go somewhere, I'll look. Travel information is not scarce. I can get it any time. Information changes. By the time I do go, the prices will have changed. So it's less wasteful and less cluttery for me to look but not take travel brochures until I have a better idea when I will travel."

2. They're free!

"The brochures are not free *to me*. They will consume my time and space. I will need to carry them, put them places (in the car, at home) and file them so I can find them again. It's easier for me to leave them here. Let someone else look at them. If I take then toss them, I waste paper. The business that printed them will need to print more needlessly. That costs money. It's best for everyone if I look, but don't take!"

Helen's Hint:
We tell children: "Look, but don't touch!"
Tell yourself: "Look, but don't take!"

Ninety percent of the game is half mental.

Yogi Berra

CHAPTER 6

The Feelings
That Keep You Stuck

———◦———

There is a tricycle in man. He knows, he feels and acts.
He has emotion, intellect and will.
He must develop head, heart and hand.

Sivananda (b.1887)

———◦———

INTRODUCTION

Our feelings, together with our thoughts, shape our lives. Negative feelings have a negative effect on our motivation and our actions. Negativity keeps us stuck.

Our feelings about an item can either keep us holding on to it or form the basis for letting it go. Most clutter is not physically difficult to let go of. It's not the item that looms large, but what it represents to us. When we clear out the cobwebs of emotional clutter, we will be able to let the physical item go.

When we see clutter, our negative emotions upset us. We don't want to face items that raise these feelings in us, so we make excuses and close the door on the clutter to avoid the feelings. Avoiding our feelings, however, does not make the feelings or the item go away. We keep ourselves stuck in our interwoven mental, emotional and physical clutter.

Let's unmask the feelings that keep you stuck in clutter.

Happiness does not depend on outward things,
but on the way we see them.

Leo Tolstoy

READER'S EXERCISE

Sit quietly with your eyes closed. In your mind's eye, go through your house. Picture your clutter. Look in every room. Include closets, the attic, basement and garage.

Answer this question: How do you feel when you see it?

1. Circle any and all of your feelings on the following list. A line is added at the end of each column so you can add any feelings not on the list.

2. Put an asterisk in front of the five you feel most often when you see your clutter.

afraid	divided	lost	stubborn
agitated	embarrassed	mad	stuck
alone	empty	melancholy	stunned
ambivalent	exhausted	miserable	stupid
angry	fearful	nervous	tense
annoyed	foolish	numb	terrible
anxious	frightened	obligated	terrified
ashamed	frustrated	obsessed	threatened
bored	greedy	out-of-control	tired
burdened	guilty	out-numbered	trapped
cautious	helpless	overwhelmed	troubled
challenged	hopeless	possessive	unappreciated
childish	incompetent	powerless	uncomfortable
comfortable	inpatient	pressured	uneasy
confused	insecure	sad	unhappy
defeated	intimidated	safe	upset
desperate	isolated	scared	vulnerable
discouraged	lazy	secure	wasteful
distracted	lonely	sneaky	worried
_____	_____	_____	_____

OVERWHELMED – The Number One Response

Why does clutter overwhelm us?

Our things outnumber us – Americans own thousands, tens of thousands of things. Each one calls for a decision. That's an overwhelming task.

When you see all of your clutter at one time, you overwhelm yourself with the magnitude of the situation. Learn to focus on one item at a time.

Clutter didn't come into your life all at one time. De-cluttering would be overwhelming if you tackled all at once. It also would be overwhelming if you had to learn everything from grades one through twelve in one year, rather than in twelve years of school. We learn over time. We de-clutter over time.

We desire instant gratification. We want our needs met NOW! – fast food, fast cars, fast communication. We want our clutter gone NOW! Our attention span, our interests wane over time, but . . .

De-cluttering takes time. **There is no quick fix.**

We all feel overwhelmed at times. When you do, take a quick time out. Give yourself space to take a few deep breaths.

Picture how you want the situation to be and think of a small action to get there. Then take action. **The antidote for anxiety is action.**

 Helen's Hint: You created the overwhelming conditions. You can change those conditions. When overwhelmed, focus. Find three small things you can toss. Don't compound the feeling with inaction. Act. Toss them now!

A day of worry is more exhausting than a day of work.

John Lubbock

STRATEGIES TO PREVENT FEELING OVERWHELMED

🏵 Set specific objectives.

🏵 Take small, realistic, measurable steps.

🏵 Pretend you have on blinders. Stay focused.

🏵 Example steps:

- "When I get the mail, I'll decide immediately what's junk mail and throw it out the first time I handle it."

- "After I get dressed, I'll hang up my robe on the hook in the bathroom where it belongs, rather than throw it on the bed, then hang it up."

✎ READER'S EXERCISE

Get Specific About Your Clutter

If asked what clutters your life, would you say "books" or "clothes" or "paper?" Don't generalize! One key to successful de-cluttering is to be specific in describing your clutter. Books aren't clutter. But, some books may become clutter, such as:

- Books on the stairs that you trip over every day.
- Books that you have read once, and will never read again.
- Books that are in the way of the ones you want to read.
- Old text books

Reader, what clutters your life? Jot down three things. Be specific!

1. _____

2. _____

3. _____

The person who moves a mountain begins by carrying away small stones.

Chinese Proverb

REASSURANCE!

 You have the ability to out-think and out-last any *thing* you own.

 Your clutter ONLY has numbers on its side – nothing else.

 Because <u>you</u> created the overwhelming numbers, you <u>can</u> reduce them.

 If you give up the futile attempt to acquire things to fill needs that things cannot fill; and let go of things to attain your higher priority of de-cluttering your life, this will be the last time clutter will overwhelm you.

 If you feel like waving "Goodbye" as clutter leaves your house, you have my permission.

Helen's Hint:
It's okay to stop reading to de-clutter
a few items now if you have the urge.

LET'S DO THE MATH!

Are you one of those "nay-sayers" who think you can't do much in 15 minutes?

Do the math!

If you spend 15 minutes a day for six days de-cluttering (take Sunday off) that totals 90 minutes a week (15 x 6 = 90 minutes). Here's the math.

90 minutes x 50 weeks (2 weeks off) = 4,500 minutes or 75 hours a year. WOW!

The next time you think that you can't do much in 15 minutes, think again! Do the math! Your time and efforts add up!

Without discipline, there's no life at all.

Katherine Hepburn

FEAR OF LOSS

When we are attached to owning and possessing things, we live in fear of losing what we possess. With attachment comes fear. You can't have one without the other.

We become attached to things for different reasons, such as security or sentiment. We think if we let go of the thing, we will lose what it represents.

It's hard to embrace change when we fear we will end up in a losing position. Fear messages used by the media to market products add to our own fears.

Sometimes we fear loss more than we should. We often place more significance on a loss than a gain. Would you be twice as unhappy about losing a watch as you would be pleased about getting a watch? Or a sweater? Or a book? Or a dollar?

The key? Recognize you are afraid. Find a process that minimizes fear so when fear bubbles up, you're able to de-clutter in spite of it. This book offers such a process.

You gain strength, courage, and confidence by every
experience in which you really stop to look fear in the face.
You are able to say to yourself, "I lived through this horror.
I can take the next thing that comes along."

Eleanor Roosevelt

 READER'S EXERCISE

Reader, what do you fear losing? List your fears. Examples: I'm afraid I'll end up with nothing. I'm afraid I'll get frustrated and quit.

I am afraid that: _____

I am afraid that: _____

I am afraid that: _____

REASSURANCE

- Letting go does **not** mean losing *every* thing you own, or *any* thing you treasure.

- Letting go does **not** mean you will end up with nothing.

- Letting go does **no**t mean you "have to" give up any item.

- Fear keeps us from looking beyond loss to see "the rest of the story" – what we **gain** by letting go, such as: the good feelings that can reinforce letting go habits, a clarity of what is really important in your life, the refusal to settle for a quantity of mediocre or meaningless things.

- Just as clutter is on three levels (physical, mental and emotional) you benefit on all three levels from de-cluttering. You *may* end up with fewer physical items, but that will be balanced by gains on the mental and emotional levels.

- You benefit on the physical level, too – physical exercise, added safety, more space for friends, family, fresh air – life!

READER, REASSURE YOURSELF

1. Look at the fears you listed. Are you willing to acknowledge them, yet set them aside to keep reading and doing the exercises in this book? ☐ Yes ☐ No

2. Choose one fear. Think about it for a moment. Can you reassure yourself that it probably will not happen? For example, if you were afraid you will end up with nothing, reassure yourself that (reading above) "letting go does not mean I'll end up with nothing."

Choose one fear. List it here.

_____

Reassure yourself:

_____

If you wait for the perfect moment when all is safe and assured, it may never arrive.
Mountains will not be climbed, races won, or lasting happiness achieved.

Maurice Chevalier

TIME TO LIGHTEN UP!

A DIFFERENT PERSPECTIVE:

Your Clutter's Point of View

Your clutter didn't come into your home on its own and it isn't going to leave on its own. Why should it **voluntarily** leave?

Your clutter spends more time in your house than you spend. You go to work to support it while it stays put and lounges all day. (Oh, no! Couch clutter!) While you shovel the snow off the sidewalk, your clutter enjoys the cozy, warm environment of your home. Does it offer to shovel snow for you? No! Does it warm your car for you? No!

While you mow the lawn in the hot summer sun, your clutter enjoys the refreshing cool environment inside your home. Does it mow for you? No! Rake for you? No! Does it make a cool drink for you? No!

Does it have dinner ready when you get home from a hard day at the office? No. Does it do the laundry? Vacuum? No, No! **You** work - your clutter sits home. What *does* it do all day? It enjoys *every minute* of being couch clutter in your house!

Why would your clutter want to be homeless? It has all the benefits of living in your house without *any* work. Wouldn't you like to have that – benefits without work?

Would *you* want to be tossed in a trash bag and put out on the sidewalk? No! Neither does your clutter. What your clutter does all day is plan how to get you to do nothing about getting rid of it. Your inertia allows your clutter to live in comfort **with you.**

Next time you pick up an item to let go and have second thoughts, think again! See how effective your clutter is in planting seeds of doubt and fear in your head and heart? The doubt and fear keep you stuck holding on to your clutter.

Clutter is fighting for its life! But you're fighting for your life, too.

A life *without* clutter.

EMPTINESS

How will you fill your life if not with things?

We came into this world empty; from empty, we could grow and learn. Along the road, we bought into the illusion that things were more than things. But that thought is not true. Worldly possessions cannot fill emptiness – they only fill space.

When we buy a house, it's empty. From that emptiness, we can make that space our own. Cluttering our space often expresses an internal emptiness which we try to fill outside ourselves with things. Clutter distracts us from facing the emotional void. When we fill the internal void, our need to fill space diminishes.

Consider:

⮡ It's time that you treasure yourself, rather than collect treasures.

⮡ It's time you acknowledge and appreciate your self worth, rather than the dollar amount of any object.

⮡ It's time you see the abundance in living, not collect an abundance of things.

⮡ It's time you replace caring for inanimate objects with caring for yourself. It's your turn to live and grow.

Riches are not from abundance of worldly goods,
but from a contented mind.

Mohammed

REASSURANCE

• Emptiness, like fullness, has a purpose in our lives.

• Emptiness is a temporary place. It will pass.

• Emptiness is a part of life. It's nothing to fear.

• Emptying space makes room for you to fulfill yourself in a more meaningful way.

CONSIDER THIS:

Dr. Wayne W. Dyer, in his book, *Real Magic*, (Copyright © 1992, p. 71-71) encourages us to become comfortable with the idea that emptiness (he refers to "nothingness") has something to offer. He draws from Robert Frost's words:

"We dance around in a ring and suppose,
But the secret sits in the middle, and knows."

Dr. Dyer then explores the meaning to this "secret in the center."

He starts by asking us to consider that it's the space between the notes that makes the music. Music is not one note or even a series of notes. Silent, empty space between the notes is required to have music. A note without silence just keeps sounding. Nothingness is absolutely necessary in order to create sound. "No nothingness, no music."

He then asks us to consider that a room is not room without silent empty space within. The room "is not the mortar, wood, or beams that make up the material part of the room. Put it all in a heap and you have no room. You must have that silent empty invisible space surrounded by all that form in order to have a room. No nothingness, no room."

LETTING GO AND FAMILY

Did you circle "safe" or "comfortable"on the list? We connect family, love, comfort and safety with clutter because for many of us, clutter was a part of the environment in which we were raised. We link clutter with childhood and family.

Many of our parents and/or grandparents were raised during the Depression and experienced rationing during World War II. Because items were scarce, our parents (or our grandparents) valued things. When things became plentiful again, they gathered possessions around them in order to soothe the memories from past deprivations.

We who are children of depression-era parents benefitted from their experiences. We were given a lot of things. Our parents didn't want us to go without things like they did. Things comforted our parents. They passed that connection of things with comfort to us.

➥   You may have been raised by pack rats, but that does not mean you have to continue that life style in order to hold on to the comfort and safety of childhood and family.

➥   The choice to live clutter-free need not be a rejection of your parents' lifestyle.

➥   You can live clutter-free and have a comfortable home of your own.

➥   Clutter was the comfort zone of your parents/grandparents. Make your own comfort zone. Clutter isn't comfortable for you, or you wouldn't be reading this book.

✎ READER'S EXERCISE

List three ways you benefitted from your parents or grandparents experience of scarcity.

1. _____

2. _____

3. _____

Read the statements aloud. Thank your parents and/or grandparents. Let's move on.

MY EXAMPLES OF GETTING UNSTUCK

Example 1.

When I practiced law, I had closets full of clothes. After law, when I looked at the clothes, I was facing my thoughts and feelings about no longer practicing law. I couldn't let them go because I thought maybe I'd wear them if I practiced law again. So long as I held on to the clothes, I could protect myself in case I changed my mind. If I got rid of the clothes did that mean that I couldn't go back to practicing law? That was scary. I could avoid the fear of change if I kept the clothes "just in case."

However, holding on also prevented me from entering fully into my new life. I was keeping myself partially in my past, not fully letting go.

My thoughts and feelings kept me stuck. That stuck-ness was manifested by the clothes. I started to question my "hold on" thoughts and feelings. By the time I might wear those clothes, would they be in style? Would I be the same size? Was keeping the "just in case" clothes the best I could do for me? No!

I reminded myself that the letting go process was not "all or nothing," or all at once! It was some items now, some later and some not at all. It was a selection process. I culled my clothing then and two times each year. I let go of some clothing right away, some more each time over the years. I have kept three dresses and one suit that I would enjoy wearing again.

As I let go of clothing and saw that my life didn't fall apart, I moved farther away from my limiting thoughts and fears. I made room for new clothes that better fit my new life.

Example 2.

When I left law in 1989, I brought home three full boxes. One box contained personal items, such as photographs. Two boxes were full of papers I wanted to keep. Once a year I applied the selection process that had worked for me with clothes. Each year some of the papers became less important to me. I allowed the distance that time brings to influence my decision making. The key component in my process was reviewing and culling the boxes yearly. The result? I've kept 1/3 of one box – the cream of the crop.

DE-STRESS REMINDER

Clutter is a stressor. Chapters 4, 5 and 6 unmask the stresses of clutter. You reduce that stress by de-cluttering your life. The next chapter shows you how much you have already accomplished.

Note: If an item brings up a feeling that makes you hesitate to let it go and you find you cannot work through the feeling, don't force yourself. This is a de-clutter de-stress process. Turn your attention away from the item you are stuck on and turn it toward something you can get rid of – something less emotional, something easier. The point is to not stop moving forward.

Leo Buscaglia
The Natural Flow of Love

My mother, on her death bed, chastised me for crying. "What are you holding on to?" she asked. At that moment I was too shocked and saddened to allow the wisdom of her words to settle in my mind. Later, though, I came to understand that she was telling me to get on with life. Her time had passed while most of mine still lay ahead.

I've let go of many things since then and it has made all the difference. I recently moved from a home in which I had lived for over forty years. Memories of joy, pain, beauty, dreams, people and adventures filled every closet and every drawer of every room. I thought I would never be able to abandon this home to strangers.

But, recalling Mama's question, I simply closed the door and left. It was so simple. I realized that the memories and dreams I valued were not hanging in the closets or hiding in the drawers; they were in me and I would be taking them wherever I went.

It's very human to cling to what we have, but in so doing, we destroy the natural ebb and flow of life.

CHAPTER 7

How Are You Doing?

---

*It isn't for the moment you are
stuck that you need courage,
but for the long uphill climb back to
sanity, and faith and security.*

Anne Morrow Lindberg

AT THIS POINT, YOU HAVE ACCOMPLISHED THE FOLLOWING:

✔ Check off each point you have accomplished!   YES!

❋ **Distinguished three processes: de-clutter, organize and simplify**   ❏

❋ **Assessed your history with clutter**   ❏

❋ **Acknowledged that you created your clutter**   ❏

❋ **Written your "Headline"**   ❏

❋ **Understand what your clutter is**   ❏

❋ **Checked the prices you pay for your cluttered lifestyle**   ❏

❋ **Unmasked your cluttering self-talk**   ❏

❋ **Unmasked your cluttered feelings**   ❏

❋ **Taken steps to prevent feeling overwhelmed.**   ❏

❋ **Listed some of your fears and reassured yourself**   ❏

❋ **Thanked your parents and grandparents**   ❏

BRAVO !!

Simplification of outward life is not enough. It is merely the outside. But I am starting with the outside. I am looking at the outside of a shell, the outside of my life – the shell. The complete answer is not to be found on the outside, in an outward mode of living. This is only a technique, a road to grace. The final answer, I know, is always inside. But the outside can give a clue, and help one to find the inside answer. One is free, like the hermit crab, to change one's shell.

Anne Morrow Lindbergh
Gift From the Sea © 1955

CHAPTER 8

Success Essentials

—————⇒ο⇐—————

If no one ever took risks,
Michelangelo would have painted
the Sistine floor.

Neil Simon

—————⇒ο⇐—————

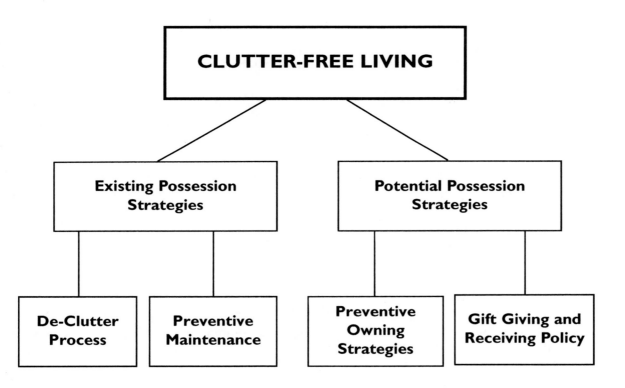

TO LIVE A CLUTTER-FREE LIFE, YOU MUST:

1. Control Existing Possessions, and

2. Prevent Future Clutter.

1. Control Existing Possessions
Two key components:

- **De-Cluttering Possessions**
  Getting rid of clutter. This is the "catch-up" part of the process.

- **Preventive Maintenance**
  Preventing possessions you use from becoming clutter by developing daily maintenance habits. It's the "keep-up" part of the process.

2. Prevent Future Possessions
Two key components:

- **Preventing Ownership**
  Re-framing your cluttery self talk to prevent you from acquiring things unnecessarily. This technique is directed at you.

- **Gift Giving and Receiving Policy**
  This component helps you operate in the world in a de-cluttered manner. It prevents you from giving clutter to or receiving clutter from others. This technique is directed at other people.

A combination of all of these are essential to successful clutter-free living.

What makes them happen? Your commitment of time. Clutter management and time management go hand in hand. You can't have one without the other.

The difference between the impossible and the possible lies in determination.

Tommy Lasorda

CHAPTER 9

The Clutter/Time Relationship

For everything there is a season, and a time for every matter under heaven:
a time to be born and a time to die;
a time to plant and a time to pluck up what is planted;
a time to kill and a time to heal; a time to break down and a time to build up;
a time to weep and a time to laugh; a time to mourn and a time to dance;
a time to cast away stones and a time to gather stones together;
a time to embrace and a time to refrain from embracing;
*a time to seek and a time to lose; a time to keep and **a time to cast away**;*
a time to rend and a time to sew; a time to keep silence and a time to speak;
a time to love and a time to hate; a time for war and a time for peace.

[Emphasis added]

Ecclesiastes 3:1-8

INTRODUCTION

Dost thou love life?
Then do not squander time, for that's the stuff life is made of.

Ben Franklin

THE LANGUAGE OF TIME

Our language implies that we can find time, lose time, save time and make time, but we can do none of these.

Our language implies that time can fly or time can drag. Not so.

We cannot control the march of time. Ignoring clutter does not put extra time in our time banks to spend on some other activity without a time pay back.

Ownership of things requires we spend time on them. The more we own, the more time we must spend on them.

PEOPLE WHO CLUTTER – AND TIME

Generally, people with clutter have a poor sense of time when it comes to possessions.

We buy too early. We aren't sure we need the item, but we buy it "just in case."

We hold on too long. We spent "good money" on an item so we keep it beyond its useful time (it becomes out-of-date or damaged) and therefore

We let go too late. We forget we own it, can't find it or can't give it away any longer because it has become unusable. Sigh.

Don't let yesterday use up too much of today.

Will Rogers

A TIME PEP TALK (Rah, Rah!)

Managing things takes time. Managing time (yourself) requires your possessions be organized, so you can find them when you want them, with a minimum of effort.

Do you tell yourself, "I don't have time to deal with my clutter"?

It's not a question of "having" time. It's a question of how much time and when you'll take time for it. Use the strong action verb "take," not the weak "have." Take time.

Do you tell yourself, "I'll do it later (tomorrow, someday)" ?

When you put off de-cluttering things today, you add to the piles for "later" and increase the amount of time you will need then. You don't make progress – you need more time to catchup because you are now farther behind. It's hard enough to keep up, without having to catchup. You'll not have "more" time later. Take time to make time.

Do you tell yourself, "I have more important things to do" ?

Yes, there are more important things to do, but that doesn't mean you give no time to de-cluttering. It's not all or nothing! Put de-cluttering in the same category as brushing your teeth - it's not fun, but it's necessary. It doesn't take long because you do it daily.

When you put off de-cluttering, you create time debt. As with credit card debt, you spent the money and now you pay interest on it; with clutter, you've spent the time. Now you pay the principal time plus time interest so it takes longer. It's pay back time.

Do you tell yourself, "I won't start until I can finish"?

You have it in reverse. You won't finish until you start.

*I stopped whining about not having enough time when
I realized that we all have 24 hours a day.*

Wanda Rosseland

RE-THINK TIME AND IMPORTANCE

When you spend time in 2001 looking through a 1995 magazine to see if there is anything "important" in there, you waste current minutes. Importance is relative. If the recipe in there was important, you would have cooked it by now. What makes it more important to look through the magazine now than when it came in? Nothing.

The question is: How important is it **now!** If you had de-cluttered the magazine in 1995, you wouldn't be looking at it now. At this point in time, your time is more important.

Would you want your physician to read three-year old medical information? No! Why are you reading yours to decide whether to toss it! It is not worth your time. Most items become less important over time. They become out of date as time marches on. The time for it is past.

When you de-clutter old stuff spend as little time as possible. This is catch-up time. You won't catch up at a slow pace.

Quicken your pace. Check the date on the item. If old, toss it out. Move on.

We are now faced with the fact that tomorrow is today. We are confronted with the fierce urgency of now. In this unfolding conundrum of life and history there is such a thing as being too late. Procrastination is still the thief of time... Over the bleached bones ...are written the pathetic words: 'Too late.' There is an invincible book of life that faithfully records our vigilance or our neglect....

Where Do We Go from Here: Chaos or Community?
© 1967, Rev. Dr. Martin Luther King, Jr.

HABITS and TIME

De-Cluttering Your Life Is like Brushing Your Teeth

Would you consider brushing your teeth only once a week so you could spend less time brushing? No! Is it good for you? No. Let's add up your minutes brushing (3 x a day @ 3 minutes a time x 7 days = 63 minutes). Brushing for 63 minutes at one time would be a drag! Brushing once a week, when we eat every day, isn't going to sustain our teeth for the long haul. We brush 2-3 times a day for a few minutes each a time, each day, every day, without excuse. That's the best for the health of our teeth.

De-cluttering once a week, when we handle things every day, won't get the job done.

Do you take a day off every week from brushing your teeth? No! Do you not brush during vacation? No! Do you plan to stop brushing? No!

It's the same with de-cluttering your life. De-clutter every day, a few times a day, every day of your life, like teeth brushing. You will never stop. There will be something to toss out or give away every day of your life, for the rest of your life.

Even though we brush our teeth daily, we schedule time with the dentist at least twice a year for a checkup and cleaning. We may not like going to the dentist, but we go.

De-clutter every day and schedule a clutter checkup at least twice a year. Spring cleaning and getting ready for winter holidays, are examples of two good times.

Although chronic procrastinators have their own idiosyncratic ways of putting things off, they all have certain traits and experiences in common. First and foremost, they're filed with good intentions about accomplishing things that are important to them. However, as Will Rogers once said, "Even if you're on the right track, you'll get run over if you just sit there."

Dr. Linda Sapadin © 1996
It's About Time

POOR HABITS CONSUME TIME

Each time you handle an item, you choose to handle it in a de-cluttered or cluttered way.

You can hang up your coat once or hang it up twice -- you can hang it in the closet the first time or hang it on a chair then put it in the closet later, thereby hanging it up twice. You sort the mail once, or get the mail, drop it on the table, change your clothes, pick up the mail again, leaf through it, drop it down while starting dinner, then pick it up again and begin to go through it more seriously. The cluttered way consumes time.

HABIT

I am your constant companion.
I am your greatest helper or your heaviest burden
I will push you onward or drag you down to failure.
I am completely at your command.
Half the things you do, you might just as well turn over to to me,
And I will be able to do them quickly and correctly.
I am easily managed; you must merely be firm with me.
Show me exactly how you want something done,
And after a few lessons I will do it automatically.
I am the servant of all great men
And, alas, of all failures as well.

Those who are great, I made made great.
Those who are failures, I have made failures.
I am not a machine, though I work with all the precision of a machine
Plus the intelligence of a man.
You may run me for profit, or run me for ruin;
It makes no difference to me.
Take me, train me, be firm with me
And I will put the world at your feet.
Be easy with me, and I will destroy you.
Who am I?
I am HABIT!

Author Unknown
quoted from *The Ten Natural Laws of Time and Life Management*
by Hyrum Smith ©1994

 **READER'S EXERCISE**

Circle one of each of the group of four sentences which best represents you.

Putting Things Where They Belong:

1 I usually put things where they belong the first time.
2. Usually, I put things down somewhere, then put them away later.
3. Usually I put things down and heaven knows if and when they will be put away.
4. Put away? Duh! What does that mean?

Picking Up After Yourself:

1. I pick up after myself every day so I can start each day fresh, without having to clean up from the previous day.
2. I pick up after myself a few times a week, but I have no routine and I do it only when I have a higher goal, like finding something that's missing.
3. I pick up after myself once a week. Isn't that what Saturday morning is for?
4. Pick up after myself? Duh! What does that mean?

Handling Things:

1. I see what you mean. I choose to handle things in a cluttered or de-cluttered way.
2. I'm not convinced that it's my decision to handle something in a cluttered or de-cluttered way. I just do what comes naturally at the moment.
3. I don't handle anything. That's my mother's/wife's/spouse's job.
4. Handle things? Duh. What does that mean?

Habits:

1. I see now that the repetitious cluttering habits I have can add up to wasted time. It's time I get more conscious about what I do with my things.
2. Sure, I have a cluttering habit now and then, but I usually am really good about how I handle things.
3. A few minutes here and there aren't going to matter. So what if they add up. I can catchup later on -- when I have more time.
4. Cluttering habits? Duh. What does that mean?

SCORE: The lowest score is 4. The highest score is 16. Total your score ___.
The lower your score, the better sense of time you have.

TIME STRATEGIES
Change Your Cluttering Habits

Time Strategy #1: Track Habits on Paper

Choose one habit you want to change. Track that habit for a week before you try to change it. Understand it first. What triggers it? What are the consequences? Keep it simple. Example habit: I throw my coat over a chair:

Day	Time	Mood	Trigger	Consequence
Wed.	6pm	rushed	had to make dinner	John put his bookbag on it and it stained.

Time Strategy #2: Practice Good Habits

Balance a cluttering habit by adding a de-cluttering habit to your repertoire. Example:

- If you haven't read a daily issue of the newspaper or unsolicited junk mail by garbage night, toss it out. (You'll get more next week!)

- Each evening, spend 15 minutes picking up items and putting them back where they belong - a place for everything, and everything in its place.

Jot one de-cluttering habit that you will adopt starting now.

- _____

Excellence is a habit. You are what you repeatedly do.

Shaquille O'Neal

Time Strategy #3: Set Start/Trigger Times

Hook de-clutter start times to life events to automatically trigger **when** you will de-clutter. Examples:

- When a new issue of a magazine or catalog arrives in the mail, toss out an older one. One in, one out!

- Each change of season (4 times a year) set aside the first Saturday morning of the new season for the entire family to handle a major de-cluttering project.

- When a drawer is hard to close or open, de-clutter the drawer contents until it closes or opens easily.

Add one of your own.

- _____

Time Strategy #4: Set Target Times

Set a deadline when you will finish a specific de-clutter project. It's easier to work toward deadlines.

Choose target times, such as a birthday, a dinner-party, a holiday. List three events within a year to use as target times to finish your de-cluttering projects. Example? I will finish de-cluttering the linen closet by Columbus Day.

	Project	Event
1.	_____	_____
2.	_____	_____
3.	_____	_____

> *Don't ask 'What if it doesn't work?'*
> *Instead ask, 'How will I feel if I don't even try?'*
>
> Suzanne Zoglio

TIME SUMMARY:

✻ The more things you own, the more time you need to devote to them.

✻ Lack of time is an excuse not to de-clutter, but wasting time is the primary reason to de-clutter. Sigh!

✻ You won't "have" time to de-clutter. You must "take" time!

✻ Time for de-cluttering is analogous to brushing your teeth. It's not fun, but it's necessary. Do it daily, without any excuses, no days off.

✻ Habits can waste time or make good use of time. The choice is yours.

✻ Strategies:
Track Bad Time Habits
Practice Good Time Habits
Set Start/Trigger Times
Set Target Times

✻ Importance is relative. Most items are less important the older they get -- especially in relation to your time.

All this will not be finished in the first hundred days.
Nor will it be finished in the first thousand days,
nor in the life of this administration,
nor even perhaps in our lifetime on this planet.
But let us begin.

John F. Kennedy
Inaugural Address, 1961

CHAPTER 10

The Sport of De-Cluttering – Practice!

Life is a romantic business.
It is painting a picture, not doing a sum –
but you have to make the romance,
and it will come to the question
how much fire you have in your belly.

Oliver Wendell Holmes, Jr.

PRACTICE MAKES POSSIBLE!

PRACTICE: The Exercise of De-Cluttering

How do first-class athletes become excellent at their sport?

PRACTICE! PRACTICE! PRACTICE!

You and I become first-class de-clutter athletes through practice, that is regular focused repetition!

The Power of Repetition

Repetition has a profound impact on us, either for good or for harm.

Advertising companies know the power of repetition. Most of us can sing a popular jingle or say an advertised slogan from continual repetition in commercials.

Champions keep playing until they get it right.

Billy Jean King

WHAT TO PRACTICE? THE BASICS

When you begin a sport, you practice basic skills repeating them until they become unconscious habits.

When you begin de-cluttering, you practice basic skills until they become new habits. The practices are easy so I call it the de-cluttering of "Easy Stuff."

If you're climbing the ladder of life, you go rung by rung,
one step at a time... Sometimes you don't think you're progressing
until you step back and see how high you've really gone.

Donny Osmond

WHEN TO PRACTICE

For physical exercise, we are advised to exercise at least 30 minutes a day, most days of the week. The 30 minutes can be broken up into shorter periods throughout the day.

It's the same with de-cluttering. Practice not in a few long marathon sessions, but daily, using bits of time.

It's easy to have faith in yourself and have discipline
when you're a winner, when you're number one.
What you got to have is faith and discipline when you're not a winner.

Vince Lombardi

BENEFITS OF PRACTICE:

* Practice prevents "creeping" clutter from taking hold.

* It hones your skills at letting go.

* It helps you combat the fear of letting go.

* It improves your decision-making ability.

* It helps you let go of limiting thoughts, such as "I can't let go!"

* It reinforces positive experiences and feelings of accomplishment.

* It helps you accept letting go as a natural part of life.

STRATEGY: USE EXISTING BITS OF TIME

Advertising companies schedule their ads. Schedule your practice. Take minutes out of existing time. Examples:

Get up from the television during commercials and de-clutter. That's about 20 minutes every hour, broken up into 3-5 minute segments.

Bring that dreaded paper work to your chair and sort it in front of the television.

Burn extra calories. Combine de-cluttering with movement – put on upbeat music and dance while de-cluttering.

Sort through magazine articles during waiting time.

Courage is very important.
Like a muscle, it is strengthened by use.

Ruth Gordon

CHAPTER 11

The Easy Stuff

———◦———

The expectations of life depend upon diligence;
the mechanic that would perfect his work
must first sharpen his tools.

Confucius

———◦———

INTRODUCTION

We have arrived at the outer skin of the onion.　　"Great!"

Would you peel the skin of an onion and keep it?　　"No! It's garbage, toss it."

Would you call it a "no brainer?"　　"Of course. I don't have to think about it."

DEFINITION OF "EASY STUFF"

"Easy stuff" is stuff that is easy for *anyone* to let go of.

- The decision to toss is easy to make - it's a "no brainer."

- There is little or no risk of making a mistake.

- There are no emotional attachments to break.

- You see quick results, especially in the space that is left.

- The time in your life for easy stuff has passed.

- It's stuff you wouldn't want people to know you kept!

- It is trash, unusable by anyone and you wouldn't think of giving it away.

[Another great task] is to confront the poverty of satisfaction –
a lack of purpose and dignity – that inflicts us all.
Too much and too long, we seem to have surrendered community excellence and
community values in the mere accumulation of material things.

Robert F. Kennedy
(as quoted in *Make Gentle The Life of This World* by Maxwell Taylor Kennedy)

TWO TYPES OF EASY STUFF:

One: DAMAGED
Two: OUT-OF-DATE

Type 1: Damaged Easy Stuff
These items have deteriorated, have become junk. They are garbage.

Where Do You Find Damaged Easy Stuff?

In basements, garages, attics, closets, storage sheds:
- Things are moldy, rusted, broken, smelly, buggy or torn beyond repair.

In the kitchen:
- Things have gone sour, are unrecognizable, smelly, freezer burned or buggy.

In the bathroom:
- Things are oozy, leaky, rusted, moldy.

Type 2: Out-of-Date Easy Stuff

An expiration date helps you make a quick decision. When the date passes, the item's goodness has expired. Its time is up – for everyone. Example:

I was de-cluttering the kitchen of a client (I'll call Celia) who was downsizing from her home to a retirement apartment. Celia's apartment kitchen would be much smaller and she would eat two meals a day at the community center. I was sorting cereal.

> Helen: "Oh, here's an unopened box of cereal!"

> *Celia: "Take it. It's still good."*

> Helen: "It's dated '1999.'"

> *Celia: "Throw it out. It's no good. I can get more."*

In What Rooms Do We Find Out-of-Date Easy Stuff?

The Bathroom, Kitchen and Home Office

PAPER EASY STUFF

In what room do we find paper easy stuff? Room?
Paper easy stuff doesn't have a room. It has a **house!**
It's all over! Hunt it down!

Examples

- Coupons and rebate offers that have expired

- Theater or meeting schedules from several years ago

- Instructions for the VCR you no longer own

- Un-opened "junk mail" you were saving to read in case there was something important in there and it now has cobwebs on it. Ugh!

- Copies of hand-made maps to your former house; out-dated maps of any kind

- Information you cut out ten years ago about a medical procedure you thought you might need but haven't had yet and may never have

- Business cards of businesses you thought you might use when you renovated the house five years ago

It doesn't matter when you start as long as you start now.

W. Edward Deming

READER'S EXERCISE

TAKE ACTION!

1. Grab garbage bags and recycle bins.
2. Choose where to start. Go there.
3. De-clutter Easy Stuff. Fill trash bags and/or a recycle bins.
4. Check off the rooms from which you remove Easy Stuff!
   Use the check list below.

 Helen's Hint: Think you don't have any easy stuff?
Humor me. Double check that you don't!
It's the practice that counts.

No more delay! Get going!
NOW!

ROOM-BY-ROOM CHECK LIST

- ☐ Basement
- ☐ Laundry
- ☐ Garage
- ☐ Kitchen:
  - ☐ Cabinets
  - ☐ Pantry
  - ☐ Refrigerator
  - ☐ Freezer
- ☐ First Floor Hall Closet
- ☐ First Floor Bathroom
  - ☐ Medicine Cabinet

- ☐ Vanity
- ☐ Storage Closet
- ☐ Living Room
- ☐ Dining Room
- ☐ Family Room/den
- ☐ Home Office
- ☐ Master Bedroom
- ☐ Master Bathroom
  - ☐ Medicine Cabinet
  - ☐ Vanity
  - ☐ Storage Closet

- ☐ Bedroom 2
- ☐ Bedroom 3
- ☐ Bathroom
  - ☐ Medicine Cabinet
  - ☐ Vanity
  - ☐ Storage Closet
- ☐ Linen Closet
- ☐ Attic
- ☐ Storage Bin/shed
- ☐ Other spaces:

READER'S EXERCISE

RESULTS:

Estimate the amount you discarded: # of trash bags _____

# of recycle bins/bags _____

I put out so much stuff, I was asked if I was moving! ☐ Yes ☐ No

List an example of what you learned from decluttering the easy stuff. Name a step you'll take to prevent future easy stuff. Example:

Lesson: I had 6 boxes of cereal and tossed 3 that were unopened but out-of-date.

Step: I'll wait until I have only one unopened box to buy more cereal.

Your Turn:

Lesson: _____

Step:_____

REVIEW YOUR ACCOMPLISHMENTS   Check if done!

* You have completed a quick purge of "easy stuff" and gotten the trash layer of clutter out of your way.   ☐

* You've made all your next steps easier.   ☐

* You have some practice under your belt.   ☐

* You conquered inertia.   ☐

* You've begun to change your life!   ☐

Hidden Benefit?

* You've taken an inventory of what you own and where your things are. ☐

Work is a great blessing;
after evil came into the world, it was given as an antidote, not as a punishment.

Arthur S. Hardy, 1923

C H A P T E R   1 2

Motivation and Support Strategies

＊━o━＊

It is good to dream, but it is better to dream and work.
Faith is mighty, but action with faith is mightier.
Desiring is helpful, but work and desire are invincible.

Thomas Robert Gaines

＊━o━＊

MOTIVATE YOURSELF TO DE-CLUTTER

Motivation means having a strong inner incentive to act with purpose in a certain direction in your life, toward your goals. Use these strategies.

Strategy # 1: Harness People Power

1-A. Interview Someone Who Has De-Cluttered His or Her Life.

Find out her motivation and process. Summarize the information here to inspire you.

Name: _____ **Date:** _____

_____

_____

_____

_____

1-B. Use Word-of-Mouth to Spread the Word

Announce that you have decided to de-clutter your life. Give a few reasons, such as you want to be able to take one thing out of a closet without everything tumbling down. **Name four people you will tell and the date you tell them.**

Name	Date	Name	Date
1. _____		3. _____	
2. _____		4. _____	

Some people say that motivation does not always last.
Well, neither does bathing – that's why we recommend it daily.

Zig Ziglar

1-C. Choose a Support Team

Ask three friends to be your support team. Explain you want to call them when you meet a goal or when you get stuck. List their names and phone numbers here.

Name   **Phone Number**

1. _____

2. _____

3. _____

1-D. Recognize: You Are Not Alone!

People de-clutter their lives and live simply for a variety of reasons. Here's a short list. Can you add more people to the list?

* Mother Theresa   * Edward VIII

* Mahatma Gandhi   * Henry David Thoreau

* Leo Tolstoy   * St. Francis

* Albert Switzer   * John Muir

* Samuel Adams   * Peter Lynch

* Buddha   * Helen Volk

* _____   * _____

All the big people are simple, as simple as the unexplored wilderness.
They love the universal things that are free to everybody.
Light and air and food and love and some work are enough.
In the varying phases of these cheap and common things,
the great lives have found their joy.

Carl Sandburg

STRATEGY #2. KEEP RECORDS OF TRIGGERING EVENTS

What experience triggered you to make an unplanned purchase? Summarize the event, the trigger and the consequences. Example:

Event: At the museum, I charged $35 at the shop for items I didn't need.

Trigger: I told myself I would look, but not buy anything. Once inside I thought I needed a memento to remember the experience of the museum. Then I thought I couldn't get something for myself without buying something for my sister.

Consequences: I spent $35 which I had planned to use to buy take-out food for dinner, then felt too guilty to spend more money to get the food. I increased the balance on my credit card. When I got home, I needed to cook dinner.

Event:

Trigger:

Consequences:

I loved what I was doing, but I came to a conclusion,
and so did some others:
What the hell are we doing this for?
I don't know anyone who wished on his deathbed
that he had spent more time at the office.

Peter Lynch, when he left Wall Street at age 47
to spend time with his children

STRATEGY #3. REWARD YOURSELF

Behavior modification requires self-discipline. How can you make it stick?

Behavior is affected by what happens afterward, so plan a prompt and reliable reward. When you procrastinate, you automatically reward yourself and reinforce your behavior in the wrong direction. Reward your performance, not the lack of it.

Example: For every hour you de-clutter, put $10 in a jar for a massage. When you save $80, go enjoy the luxury of a massage. Continue contributing for another reward.

REWARD IDEAS:

The Reward of Comfort
Cuddle with a teddy bear.
Get a massage, manicure, pedicure.
Make yourself a yummy treat.
Watch your favorite movie.
Read your favorite magazine.
Pet your pets.
Get/give a hug.
Drink a cup of hot cocoa or herbal tea.
Have warm milk and cookies before bed.
Exercise or don't exercise.
Bask in the sun.
Have a good cry.

The Reward of Laughter
Make up a funny word.
Call a friend and share a joke.
Watch a funny video movie.
Read a funny book.
Listen to a comedy tape.

The Reward of Community
Visit a zoo.
Walk through a park.
Have lunch with a friend.
Go to a live play, concert or event.
See a local historical site.
Visit an art museum.

The Reward of Creativity
Draw, paint or doodle something.
Write a letter to a friend.
Cook something new.
Work on a jig saw puzzle.
Sing a song.

The Reward of Solitude
Have a walk/talk with the Creator.
Take a hot bath.
Build a fire and sit by it.
Watch a television sitcom.
Look, really look, at a flower.

Joy is not a matter of what's happening around you, but inside you.

Steve Miller, *One Minute Promises*

STRATEGY #4. COUNT YOUR BLESSINGS

Count Your Blessings

If you woke up this morning with more health than illness . . .
you are more blessed than the million who will not survive this week

If you have never experienced the danger of battle, the loneliness of
imprisonment, the agony of torture, or the pangs of starvation . . .
you are ahead of 500 million people in the world.

If you can attend a church meeting without fear of harassment,
arrest, torture, or death . . . you are more blessed than three billion
people in the world.

If you have food in the refrigerator, clothes on your back, a roof
over head, and a place to sleep . . .
you are richer than 75% of this world.

If you have money in the bank, in your wallet, and spare change in a
dish someplace . . .
you are among the top 8 % of the world's wealthy.

If you can read this message, you are more blessed
than over two billion people in the world who cannot read at all.

E-mail Message, Author Unknown

STRATEGY #5. FIND "THE END."

De-cluttering is a means to an end. Each person listed in Strategy 1D simplified their lives for a purpose - religious, political, social, environmental, personal, etc. What do YOU want to achieve by de-cluttering YOUR life.

_____

_____

I can't believe that God put us on this earth to be ordinary.

Lou Holtz

STRATEGY #6. SPIRITUAL INFLUENCE

My commitment to live clutter free is founded in my spiritual life. Mahatma Gandhi, *The Dragon Doesn't Live Here Anymore*, the poems of Marjorie Holmes, all speak of the spiritual nature of living with few possessions.

A passage from the New Testament of the Bible speaks about the **call** to live a simple life.

"Jesus called the twelve disciples together and gave them power and authority to drive out all demons and to cure diseases. Then he sent them out to preach the Kingdom of God and to heal the sick, after saying to them, 'Take nothing with you for the trip; no walking stick, no beggar's bag, no food, no money, not even an extra shirt.'" Luke 9:1-3.

My Personal Insight

Jesus instructed the disciples to "travel lightly." Jesus acknowledged that the disciples, being human, couldn't focus totally on their missions if their minds were filled with trivial/daily concerns. In exchange for not taking any thing with them, the disciples were given the power and freedom to achieve their mission.

Picture the disciples figuring out which cloak or sandals to wear or what to eat. Their dialogue might go like this:

"What shall I wear today? Are these demon-casting out shoes? Is this a disease-curing cloak?" or "Where shall we eat? Is there a little café or deli along the way? Should we stop to catch some fish and roast our own? What spices shall we use?"

Neither you nor I can focus on our missions **and** worry about the details of everyday living.

I could put time, money and energy into dressing for a seminar, rather than preparing the message. "Is this a de-clutter seminar jacket? Are these teaching shoes?"

Yes, it *is* important how we look, but we needn't go overboard. Details of living must be kept simple so they do not distract us from our work.

What other choice is there but to have hope?

Lance Armstrong

READER'S FAITH TEACHING

Note here a teaching in your faith tradition which inspires you to de-clutter your life.

_____

_____

_____

_____

_____

ANOTHER FAITH TEACHING
(paraphrased from Luke 12: 22-34)

Jesus told his disciples: "Don't worry about what you'll eat; or what you'll wear."

Consider the ravens – They don't sow or reap, they have no storeroom or barn; yet God feeds them. How much more valuable you are than birds! Who of you by worrying can add a single hour to his life? Since you cannot do this very little thing, why worry about the rest?

Consider how the lilies grow. They don't labor or spin. Yet, not even Solomon in all his splendor was dressed like one of these. And do not worry about what you will eat or drink. God knows that you need them. Seek his kingdom, and these things will be given to you.

Don't be afraid! Sell your possessions. Give them to the poor. Provide purses for yourselves that will not wear out, a treasure in heaven where no thief comes near.

"For where your treasure is, there your heart will be also."

Reader's Faith Teaching

_____

_____

_____

_____

STRATEGY #7. CREATE A VISION

Develop a mental picture of your uncluttered space. If you can see in detail the result that you want and visit it frequently, you can learn to miss having it. That desire to have your vision helps you progress toward your goal.

Where there is no vision,
the people perish.

Proverbs 29:18

7-A Describe One De-cluttered Space in Detail.

Close your eyes. Focus on a specific room. Walk around it in your mind. See it from all angles. Look at the floor, furniture, the walls. Open any drawers. Vision your uncluttered space. What does it look like? Describe it in detail as if you were seeing a photo of it.

Name of room or area _____.

Description of my uncluttered space: _____

_____

_____

_____

_____

Hint: Use descriptive words like tidy, orderly, arranged, near, grouped, simple, basics, peaceful, homey, quiet, open, sufficient, clean, etc.

May your walls know joy;
may every room hold laughter and
every window open to great possibility

Mary Anne Radmacher

7-B. Draw a Picture of Your Uncluttered Space in the Following Space:

7-C. Un-Cluttered Feelings
How do you feel when you see the space de-cluttered? Circle all that apply:

alive	empowered	intelligent	rewarded
astounded	encouraged	joyous	safe
at ease	energized	lighthearted	satisfied
awed	enthusiastic	lucky	secure
brave	excited	merry	settled
calm	focused	nonchalant	soothed
capable	free	organized	steady
cheerful	friendly	overjoyed	strong
childlike	full	patient	successful
clean	gentle	peaceful	thankful
clever	gifted	pleased	thoughtful
comfortable	glad	positive	together
competent	good	powerful	unburdened
centered	great	present	understanding
confident	gratified	protected	upbeat
connected	gratitude	proud	useful
contented	happy	quiet	warm
daring	hopeful	receptive	wonderful
delighted	impressed	refreshed	worthy
determined	in charge	relaxed	young
ecstatic	inspired	relieved	

READER'S EXERCISE

Check off the motivational strategies that you have used.

Strategy	Used
Strategy #1: Harness People Power	
A. Interview Someone Who Has De-Cluttered His or Her Life.	☐
B. Use Word-of-Mouth to Spread the Word.	☐
C. Choose a Support Team.	☐
D. Make a Written Agreement with Your Spouse or a Friend.	☐
E. Recognize That You Are Not Alone!	☐
Strategy #2. Keep Records: Triggering Events	☐
Strategy #3. Reward Yourself	☐
Strategy #4. Count Your Blessings	☐
Strategy #5. Find "the end."	☐
Strategy #6. Spiritual Influence	☐
Strategy #7. Create a Vision	
A. Describe a De-Cluttered Space in Detail	☐
B. Draw a Picture of Your Uncluttered Space	☐
C. Un-Cluttered Feelings	☐

 Helen's Hint: Use these strategies over and over. Circle the number of the strategy that worked well for you. When you feel yourself slipping into inaction, come back here, find that number and reuse that strategy again.

Voluntary simplicity is a way of life that is compatible with Christianity, Buddhism, Hinduism, Taoism. Sufism, Zen, and many more traditions. The reason... is that simplicity fosters a more conscious and direct encounter with the world. And it is from the intimate encounter with life that there naturally arise the perennial experiences at the heart of all the world's great spiritual traditions.

Duane Elgin, *Voluntary Simplicity* © 1993

Never Alone

When I was young, my father, who was a butcher, used to take me and my brothers and sisters to help him in his store. He had a good business with mostly well-to-do customers – judges, lawyers, doctors, government officials, business people…

But despite his successful business, he never seemed concerned about material things. In the wintertime, my father wore an old overcoat with the pocket torn out. It never bothered him though my mother was forever trying to fix it. Also, he could not wear overshoes because they hurt his feet. He had ulcerated varicose veins that were painful. When there was snow on the ground he would wrap burlap around his shoes. It looked so unfashionable to say the least. I was ashamed, I couldn't even get out of the truck with him. When my father got out of the truck, an immaculately dressed judge who was a good friend commented, "That's quite an outfit you've got there, Peter!" My father smiled and replied good-naturedly, "Yes, Judge, you have to have dignity"

I asked my father one day why he dressed like that. He merely answered, "It is not what you wear that is important. It is what you are inside. Real dignity is in the beauty of your soul." I couldn't understand this way back then.

When I had to retire a number of years ago because of my health, I chose not to accept any compensation from the diocese, though I had no income. For the first time in my life I was nearly penniless… I learned it didn't take much to survive, not to live luxuriously, but to survive. But even with just the bare necessities, I had everything I needed to be happy.

One morning, I was taking a walk, and wondering what I would do for supper, since I had no money. Walking along the side of the road I thought I saw some money in the ditch. I took a closer look and there, lying in the ditch and neatly folded, was some money, just enough for supper. I could almost hear Jesus saying, "I told you not to worry, I would take care of you." Jesus was right and I could now say that from my own firsthand experience…

… The important thing is to maintain a detachment from whatever possessions we may have, whether they be great or small, and not allow ourselves to become so concerned about them that they become a serious distraction from our own inner growth. "Where you heart is there your treasure lies."

CHAPTER 13

Benefits

———⟫•◦•⟪———

When you came into this world,
You cried and everyone else Smiled.
You should so live your life that when you go,
everyone Else will cry and you will be Smiling.

Paramahansa Yogananda

———⟫•◦•⟪———

READER'S EXERCISE

Check the benefits which are meaningful for you. Add others that are not on the list.

✔ **Check the benefits which are meaningful for you. Add others that are not on the list.**

EMOTIONAL BENEFITS

❑ **I feel lighter, less burdened.**

❑ **I no longer worry about my possessions, but care for them appropriately.**

❑ **I'm glad to have people at my home, or my office.**

❑ **I argue with others about things a lot less.**

❑ **The daily stress in my life is reduced. I've regained my peace of mind.**

❑ **I feel more balanced in all areas of my life.**

❑ **I've created an easier, simpler style of living.**

❑ **I appreciate my treasures again.**

❑ _____

MENTAL BENEFITS

❑ **I remember where I put things.**

❑ **I organize things more easily.**

❑ **I can think straight.**

❑ **I find the "perfect" gift more easily.**

❑ **I have restored control over my space, time and life.**

❑ **I feel more secure - I can find things when I need them, especially in an emergency.**

❑ **I am clearer about myself and my priorities.**

❑ _____

The quest for truth must be carried out by each person individually.
It is like breathing, something which no one else can do for you.

Seyyed Hossein Nasr

TIME BENEFITS

❑ I no longer waste time looking for things.

❑ I spend less time on maintenance work.

❑ I run fewer errands.

❑ I spend less time shopping.

❑ I spend less time on change-of-season tasks.

❑ I have more time to do more important things.

❑ I am more in control of my time.

❑ _____

MONEY BENEFITS

❑ I spend less money on material things.

❑ I no longer buy two of some things because I can find what I have.

❑ I no longer buy a gadget, rather than search for one I already have.

❑ My things do not depreciate as much so I buy less.

❑ I spend less money to replace lost items.

❑ I eat at home and save on dinner out (guests, too).

❑ I have guests overnight at my home and save on hotel expenses.

❑ I save money.

❑ I buy only stuff that I use.

❑ I am out of debt.

❑ I sell my stuff at a garage sale or on consignment so I own less.

❑ I give unwanted items to charity.

❑ _____

SAFETY BENEFITS

❑ My home is safer from fire.

❑ I no longer trip and fall over stuff.

❑ I keep environmental illness to a minimum.

❑ I have discarded all poisons.

❑ I have discarded out of date medicines and foods.

❑ I no longer misplace records, documents, cash.

❑ _____

JOB BENEFITS

- ❑ I work smarter.
- ❑ I have less stress.
- ❑ I am more productive, effective.
- ❑ I feel in control at the office.
- ❑ I meet deadlines regularly.
- ❑ I no longer have disagreements with co-workers/boss over my work space.
- ❑ My work space appears professional.
- ❑ I have a reputation/perception as organized, professional.
- ❑ _____

RELATIONSHIP BENEFITS

- ❑ I have fewer disagreements with spouse/children/ parents/coworkers/boss over clutter.
- ❑ I spend more time with people.
- ❑ I spend less effort getting ready for guests/parties.
- ❑ I manage gift giving and receiving with ease and joy.
- ❑ I have stress-free, more rewarding holidays.
- ❑ _____

Total the boxes checked and added by you. _____ The more, the merrier.

Helen's Hint: If you get stuck, come back here
to read the checked boxes aloud.

*...I own no property and yet I feel that I am perhaps the richest man in the world.
For I have never been in want either for myself or for my public concerns. God has
always and invariably responded in time... It is open to the world, therefore, to laugh at
my dispossessing myself of all property. For me the dispossession has been a positive
gain. I would like people to compete with me in my contentment. It is the richest
treasure I own... The life I am living is certainly very easy and very comfortable, if ease
and comfort are a mental state. I have all I need without the slightest care of having to
keep any personal treasures. Mine is a life full of joy in the midst of incessant work. In
not wanting to think of what tomorrow will bring for me I feel as free as a bird.*

Mahatma Gandhi

BECOME A MILLIONAIRE!

Does owning a lot of things mean you are wealthy?

THE MILLIONAIRE NEXT DOOR
(The Surprising Secrets of America's Wealthy)
©1996, Thomas J. Stanley and William D. Danko

The authors, Stanley and Danko, after years of studying the wealthy, present their research: who is wealthy, who is not and how ordinary people can become wealthy.

They explain that wealth is **not** the same as income – if you make a good income and spend it all, you are not getting wealthier – you are just living high. Stanley and Danko say that *wealth is what you accumulate, not what you spend.*

How do you become wealthy? The authors say it is seldom luck, inheritance, advance degrees or even intelligence. Wealth they say, is the result of a lifestyle of hard work, perseverance, planning and most of all, self-discipline.

In the course of their investigation, the authors discovered seven common denominators among those who successfully built wealth. The first: *they live well below their means.*

Stanley and Danko do not do not define "wealth," "affluent," or "rich" in terms of material possessions. People who display a high-consumption lifestyle "have little or no investments, appreciable assets, income-producing assets, common stocks, bonds, private businesses, oil/gas rights, or timber land."

In Chapter 2 (Frugal, Frugal, Frugal) the authors define "wasteful" as a "lifestyle marked by lavish spending and hyper-consumption." They call being frugal "the cornerstone of wealth-building." The affluent answered "yes" to three questions: 1. Were your parents very frugal? 2. Are you frugal? 3. Is your spouse more frugal than you are?

frugal: not wasteful; not spending freely or unnecessarily; thrifty; economical
Synonym: see Thrifty

Webster's New World Dictionary
Second College Edition © 1974

KNOWING WHAT YOU VALUE

Suze Orman's Story

In her book, *The Courage to Be Rich* (©1999) Suze Orman says that to make clients think about what was really important, she would ask them to pretend that there was a fire coming and they had only thirty minutes to get things out of their house. What would they take?

After people and pets, the answers were a stream of sentimental things such as, wedding pictures, family scrapbooks, a meaningful piece of jewelry.

One year a fire in Oakland Hills approached Ms. Orman's home. She had little time to get out of her house and took the things that money could never replace. Items of the highest personal value to her were ones that were worthless to any other soul on earth.

When we are faced with a situation like this, we know beyond a doubt what has value to us – we know what to take and what to leave behind.

✎ READER'S EXERCISE

1. Do you live well below your means?   ❑ Yes   ❑ No
2. Were your parents very frugal?   ❑ Yes   ❑ No
    Are you frugal?   ❑ Yes   ❑ No
    Is your spouse more frugal than you are?   ❑ Yes   ❑ No
3. Do you know what items you value? If you only had thirty minutes to get out of your home what would you take? Jot down those items.

_____

_____

_____

Do you know where each and every one of the listed items is located now?
❑ **Yes**   ❑ **No** If not, make locating each item on this list a priority project.

A man's true wealth is the good he does in this world.

Mohammed *(As quoted in The Mustard Seed, July 1988)*

CHAPTER 14

Enough

————⟫•⟪————

There are two ways to get enough:
one is to continue to accumulate more and more;
the other is to desire less.

G. K. Chesterton

————⟫•⟪————

ENOUGH-NESS

Do you know when you own enough?

"Enough" is sufficiency, being satisfied with what you have. Our inner definition of "enough" will keep us on the road toward clutter free living.

There Is No Greater Sin Than Desire,
No Greater Curse Than Discontent,
No Greater Misfortune than Wanting Something for Oneself.
Therefore He Who Knows That Enough Is Enough
Will Always Have Enough.

Lao-tzu
(Forty-six, the Tao Te Ching):

How do you know when you own "enough?" *In Your Money or Your Life*, (© 1992) Joe Dominguez and Vicki Robin discuss "enough" in relation to money. They state that discovering what is enough for you is **core** to a positive relationship with money (and for the purposes of this book, with the possessions that money can buy.)

Dominguez and Robin created a "fulfillment curve" to demonstrate the relationship between the experience of fulfillment and the amount of money we spend on possessions.

From what we get, we can make a living;
what we give, however, makes a life.

Arthur Ashe

They explain that spending for fulfillment has three phases:

- First, as children our basic needs are met from outside of ourselves - food, clothing, shelter.

- Second, we go from bare necessities to some amenities such as toys, a wardrobe, a bicycle and unconsciously, we relate money with fulfillment and think that they come from outside us through things.

- Third, we go beyond amenities to luxuries, but not calling them "luxuries" - a car, going to college, sophisticated electronics.

We don't recognize that the price tag increases while the "high" wears off more quickly. We center our attention on things but not the added mental, emotional and physical burden. We reach the peak of the fulfillment curve and pass it by; it is on its way down.

What Is the Peak of the Fulfillment Curve? ENOUGH

Enough is having everything you need without anything extra to weigh you down, distract or distress you – nothing bought on time, have never used and are slaving to pay off. Having enough is appreciating and fully enjoying what you have and never purchasing anything that isn't needed and wanted.

What's Beyond Enough? CLUTTER!

Dominguez and Robin say that clutter is anything that is excess for you. It's whatever you have that doesn't serve you, yet takes up space in your world. Letting go of clutter is not deprivation. It's lightening up and opening up space. It is the taking back of joy.

God grant me the Serenity to accept the things I cannot change;
Courage to change the things I can; and
Wisdom to know the difference.

Reinhold Niebuhr

READER'S EXERCISE: YOUR KEY NUMBER

In your mind's eye, picture your clutter. Pretend that on a scale of 1 to 10, you are at 10. You're at the top of the scale because you are cluttered and do not want to own more. Number one means you own next to nothing.

Question: What number down from 10 would you choose to live a more reasonable, clutter-less life? Mark that number on the following scale. Jot it here. _____

10 ———————————————————————————————————— 1

Now very   **Own**

cluttered   **Very little**

You heard it right away. Don't modify it, judge it or pretend you didn't hear it.

Did you choose #5? If so, you indicate that you own twice the amount of things that you need to live a reasonably comfortable life. You've acquired 50% too much. Letting go of half of your things would bring you more life by removing the burden of excess things.

YOUR KEY NUMBER Jot it here, again. _____

GOAL

This number is your de-clutter goal number. If you chose five, as you go through the de-cluttering process, you strive to let go of half and keep half of your possessions. For example, if you were de-cluttering socks and started with 50 pairs of socks, your goal would be to keep about 25 pair and let go of about 25 pair.

This number is the key to your freedom from clutter. This number is not rigid, not an exact number, but the number to strive for. For some categories of things, you will keep less than your number; for other categories, you will keep more. You are seeking an overall balance.

The Sun and Moon
Are Not Mirrored in Cloudy Water,
Thus, the Almighty Cannot Be Mirrored
In a Heart That Is Obsessed by the Idea
Of Me and Mine.

Sri Ramakrishna

CHAPTER 15

Waste Not, Want Not Revisited

—⊳•◅—

All worry is atheism,
because it is a want of trust in God.

Bishop Fulton J. Sheen

—⊳•◅—

INTRODUCTION

In the past, things were precious because there were few of them. It was a waste to throw things out before they were used up or worn out. No so today.

Today, stores are everywhere. Things are plentiful and available. We have both the opportunity and the means to own a lot of possessions. What should "waste" mean to today's clutterers?

DICTIONARY DEFINITIONS OF "WASTE"

(Webster's New World Dictionary, Second College Edition,
© 1974 by William Collins & World Publishing Co., Inc)

- destroyed or ruined
- used up or spent without real need, gain or purpose; squandered
- did not put to full or proper use
- left over, superfluous or no longer of use
- excess of what can be used
- useless or profitless spending or consuming

Waste as "destroyed" or "ruined"

We hold onto things thinking we will use them again, only to find that if or when that time comes, we can't find them or they are ruined, that is, wasted. We have so many things that it is hard to take care of all of them or know where they are. We handle or store things without care or simply keep them in less than the best conditions so they become destroyed or ruined.

The foes from whom we pray to be delivered are our own passions, appetites, and follies; and against these there is always need that we should war.

Theodore Roosevelt

Waste as "obsolete" (Left over or no longer of use)

Things become out-of-date, obsolete. Once obsolete, items are not good for anyone to use. There is no market for them, even though they are "good" that is, in good condition. They are not "good" that is, useable. You can't sell them or give them away. What a waste!

Most of us would prefer to give our things away, rather than toss them. We can only give away things when they are useable. We throw out things we could have given away if we had acted sooner. Holding on to things "just in case" becomes wasteful.

Wasteful Purchases (Not put to full or proper use)

When we buy stuff "just in case," we waste at the time of purchase. The item wasn't needed at the time of purchase so the purchase, the time, money and energy spent in the act of purchasing were wasted. Holding on to the item so long as it's still "good" compounds the waste at time of purchase. We squandered when we bought and continue to squander the item's value.

"You Got to Know When to Hold Them; Know When to Fold Them."

At a conference at which I was speaking, there was a vendor show during the noon hour. Conference attendees were divided into two groups. The first group toured the vendor show while the second group ate lunch. Then the groups switched places.

On arriving at the vendor show, the second group found no bags and no goodies left. The first group had taken all of the plastic bags and filled them with the goodies. By taking more than their share, the first group deprived the second group of getting supplied.

When we waste, we deplete rather than increase resources for everyone. When one person wastes, another person wants.

We live very close together. So, our prime purposes in this life is to help others. And if you can't help them, at least don't hurt them.

Dalai Lama

Waste: A Statement of Worry?

When someone asks you if you trust in God, s/he is asking not only if you believe that God exists, but whether that belief affects the way you live.

Do you hold on to things thinking that:

- You may not be able to get them in the future?
- If you do need it, you won't be able to afford it?
- Or no one will give it to you if you can't afford to buy it?
- Or it won't be available at that time?

This thinking comes from fear of want, not having enough. It keeps you stuck and holding on.

OR

Do you say you have faith in God and therefore let go – believing that:

- If you do need an item some time in the future, it will be provided – in time.
- If you must buy an item you will have the money.
- If an item is available you will find it.
- If someone else has one, s/he will give/sell it to you.

This thinking comes from faith in the future. It allows you to let go and let God.

PROVERBS 30: 7-9

Two things I ask of You, O Lord;
do not refuse me before I die:
Keep falsehood and lies far from me;
give me neither poverty or riches,
but give me only my daily bread.
Otherwise, I may have too much and disown You
and say, "Who is the Lord?"
Or I may become poor and steal,
and so dishonor the name of my God.

[Emphasis Added]

READER'S EXERCISE

How do you waste? Answer each question, then write one step you will take to change.

1. I destroyed or ruined _____
One step to change: _____

2. I did not fully or properly use _____
One step to change: _____

3. A no-longer-used item I've held on to is _____
One step to change: _____

4. One wasteful habit is _____
One step to change: _____

In what ways does the connection between waste and faith help you to let go?

_____

_____

_____

God grant me the serenity to accept
the people I cannot change,
the courage to change the one I can,
*and the wisdom to know... **it's me!***

John G. Miller, author
QBQ! The Question Behind the Question

CHAPTER 16

How Are You Doing?

———⟫•⟪———

The Vigil

To believe something is not simply to hold an opinion;
it is to let that something sink down into the marrow of your bones
and form the structure of your life.
To believe something is to let its affirmation become the inhalation and
exhalation of your life's breath . . .
to believe something is to let it transform your life.

Wendy Wright

———⟫•⟪———

✔ **Check off each point you have accomplished!**

	YES!
Learned the four processes that are essential for de-cluttering success.	❏
Understand the direct correlation between owning possessions and time.	❏
Assessed your cluttering habits and taken steps to change them.	❏
Connected the commitment to brushing your teeth with de-cluttering your life.	❏
Understand the importance of practice to successful de-cluttering.	❏
Taken action to de-clutter your Easy Stuff.	❏
Selected strategies to motivate yourself to de-clutter.	❏
Recorded your faith teachings concerning possessions.	❏
Selected the benefits you will obtain from de-cluttering your life.	❏
Understand the connection between financial wealth and frugality.	❏
Selected your key number.	❏
Better understand how you waste.	❏

Celebrate what you've accomplished,
but raise the bar a little higher each time you succeed.

Mia Hamm

CHAPTER 17

De-Clutter Your Thoughts

*Of all the liars in the world,
sometimes the worst are your own fears.*

Rudyard Kipling

INTRODUCTION

*The significant problems we face
cannot be solved at the same level of thinking
that created them.*

Albert Einstein

LET GO OF YOUR MENTAL CLUTTER
Cross-Examine Your Thoughts

We think our thoughts must be true because we think them.
But *that* thought is *not* true.

- Your thought may be false
  (example: The earth is the center of the universe).

- Or unrealistic (I can fly. I can leap tall buildings in a single bound).

- Or a distortion produced by a bad experience in the past (Nobody likes me).

By listening to the thoughts you say to yourself at the specific moment you hesitate to let an item go, you focus on the cause of your clutter - your thinking. If you pry loose your thinking, you can release the item. By examining your holding-on thoughts, you

- Question if the thought is true for you **now** and

- Then work to revise it, adopt a different thought or diminish its powers so you are able to let the item go.

*One does not become enlightened by imagining figures of light,
but by making the darkness conscious.*

C.G. Jung

FOUR CROSS-EXAMINING TECHNIQUES

1. Produce the Evidence!

Get the facts. Check out your experience!

> *"What is the evidence for this thought?*
> *Is what I am telling myself true? Is it accurate?"*
> *As Jack Webb said in Dragnet: "Just the facts."*

Example: You tell yourself, "I can't throw things out." (an all encompassing thought)

Produce the Evidence. Challenge your can't-throw-things-out thought with your experience:

"I throw things in the trash **every day**. I put out garbage bags and recyclable containers **every week**. Of course I can toss things out. The thought is untrue! I do throw things out. I don't give myself credit for what I do throw out!"

> *Facts are stubborn things; and whatever may be our wishes, our inclinations, or the dictates of our passions, they cannot alter the state of facts and evidence.*
> John Adams

2. Find an Alternative Thought!

You may be choosing to de-clutter the most emotionally charged item in a category. Change your focus. Go from a general category to a specific item!

Ask yourself: *"What item in this category **can** I let go of?"*

Example: You tell yourself, "I can't let go of books." (a general category)

1. Produce the Evidence. Challenge the thought with your experience: "I have gotten rid of some books. So, the thought isn't *generally* true. I can let some books go."

2. Find an Alternative Thought. Focus on the troublesome book that generated the doubting thought in the first place. *"This one book is especially difficult to let go of because of the inscription. I know the author and want her signature."* Ask yourself: *"What item in this category can I let go of?"*

Change your focus. Find an easier specific alternative, like this:
"What book can I let go of? I've gotten rid of my high school text books. They're out of date and no one wants them. I'll focus on my college textbooks, instead of this special book. That's a workable alternative."

 Helen's Hint: This is a "don't quit strategy." Change your thought so you can find an item to de-clutter and keep going.

3. So What?

Maybe your thought is true.

Ask yourself: *"Even if my thought is correct, so what?"*

Example: You tell yourself: *"I was given this dictionary in sixth grade as a prize for the highest score in a spelling contest."* You produce the evidence and know it's true for you.

Continue to question yourself:
*"So what? Is that a reason to keep the dictionary **now**?"*

Question the importance of the item **now**, even if your thought is correct. Importance is relative. Here are some realities which put that correct, but holding-on thought in its proper place:

• I won the contest in sixth grade. That won't change if I toss out the dictionary.
• I had forgotten I had the dictionary. It can't be that memorable.
• I never look at it – it's outdated. I have spell check and a more recent dictionary.
• In relation to other prizes I have won, this one has little value to me.
• So what if it was a prize. It's not a prize to me – now!

 Helen's Hint: This technique puts importance in perspective, weighs the past against the present to test the value of the item to you – now!

4. Take the High Road

What if the thought is true, you considered alternatives and have justified keeping the item with the "so what?" technique? What then? Consider taking the road less cluttered! Let the item go for a higher purpose, one outside of yourself.

Example: You tell yourself: *"I can use these extra utensils when I have company."*

You produce the evidence from personal experience and conclude:
"That's true. Extra utensils come in handy some times. I do have dinner parties occasionally and have used these utensils."

Go one more step. Think outside of yourself. Put yourself in someone else's shoes:

"But, there was a big flood south of here last week and many people lost their homes and all their possessions. There's a local drive to collect things to help them. A large truck is parked at the mall to collect items. They ask is that the items be put in bags and be in good, clean condition. These utensils are. So, I'll contribute them to the drive. I can always get more utensils… That's a good decision. It feels right. I'll take the road less cluttered."

There is no happiness for people at the expense of other people.

Anwar Sadat

CROSS-EXAMINATION EXAMPLE

The situation: While cleaning out a closet, you find a box of clothing you had forgotten you had. You recognize each item as something you wore in the past. You hesitate to let go of the clothes because you are afraid you will lose the memories and you think to yourself, "Maybe I'll wear them again, someday" (once I lose weight).

I. Produce The Evidence:

• I hadn't opened the box in three years. I didn't know the box was there.

• The clothes must be at least four sizes smaller than I am now. I can't wear them.

• When is "someday?" Why would I think I'd wear them again?

• It's a waste to keep them in a box on a shelf.

2. Find Alternative Thoughts:

• Maybe I'll wear them in the future, then again, maybe I won't.

• I can't be too concerned about "memories" if I haven't opened the box in three years. I could take photographs of the clothes, then give them away.

• I'm afraid if I get rid of the clothes it means I've given up my dream of losing weight. What? Just because I let clothes go doesn't prevent me from losing weight in the future.

• I could keep a few favorites as an incentive to lose weight and let go of the rest. This isn't "all or nothing."

• By letting them go, I'll make room for new clothes. Once I lose weight, I'll want something new.

Nothing could be more tragic than for men to live in these revolutionary times and fail to achieve the new attitudes and the new mental outlooks that the new situation demands.

Rev. Dr. Martin Luther King, Jr.

3. So what?

- I haven't started to lose weight. When I do, who knows where on my body I'll lose it? I probably won't be four sizes smaller again. The clothes still may not fit!

- By the time I lose weight, the clothes will be outdated for ME.

- I wore these clothes once. Nothing will change that.

- Keeping the clothes won't bring back size five.

4. High Road:

- Someone else could use these clothes. If I wait too long, the clothes could deteriorate and they'll become outdated for everyone. I don't want to waste them.

- It'd be nice to know that someone is enjoying clothes that were precious to me.

- I'll act as if I weren't afraid to let go. I'll step out in faith and donate them.

A simpler life-style is not the only reward. Freeing goods for the benefit of others brings great joy. One dismally gray Sunday was brightened by a friend wearing new clothing sewn from fabric that had burdened by closet and my mind for years.

Judith Loback
"Do You Need a Larger Barn?"
magazine and date unknown

READER'S EXERCISE

Think of an item you are holding on to. Choose one thought that keeps you stuck. Cross-examine it so you are able to let the item go.

Item: _____

Holding on thought: _____

1. Produce the Evidence:

_____

_____

2. Find Alternatives:

_____

_____

3. So What?

_____

_____

4. Take the High Road:

_____

_____

Revised thought: _____

_____

Result: _____

*Consider your possessions
loaned to you by God.*

St. Catherine of Siena
(1347-1380)

CHAPTER 18

Project Process

This is no time for ease and comfort.
It is the time to dare and endure.

Winston Churchill

CHOOSE AND COMPLETE DE-CLUTTERING PROJECTS

I. CHOOSE A CATEGORY OR AREA

Start with a small, manageable area or category. Follow Julius Caesar's advice: divide and conquer! Keep de-clutter projects from becoming overwhelming by breaking them into small pieces. Concentrate on one project until it's done.

Think Globally, Act Locally (Think Goal, Act Small)

Goal: I want to de-clutter my clothing.
Act on a smaller category: the sock drawer, scarves, t-shirts or shoes, etc.

What Is "Small?"

Small is a project you can finish in *one de-clutter* session.

Ask yourself: Can I empty the entire space of the project, de-clutter it, then put back the items I want within the amount of time I have?" If not, the project is too big for the time you've allotted. Break it down into smaller units or choose something else.

 Helen's Hint: Always examine your project choice in light of the time you allot. Finish what you start.

It is the greatest of all mistakes to do nothing because you can only do a little. Do what you can.

Sydney Smith

2. DEDICATE AN AMOUNT OF TIME

Plan: Allot the time to get your project done.

Calendar-ize

Put your time commitment on your calendar. Write the letter "c"(for clutter) or your name. Why? If we see a blank space in the calendar we think we are "free." But if we see a notation on the calendar, we can answer (with authority) when asked if we are free, "No, I already have a commitment."

Key Tool: A Timer

Set a timer, one that ticks off each second. So long as it ticks, you work. You will concentrate and get more done.

3. BE PREPARED WITH

- A trash and/or recycle bag.
- A beverage.
- A pad and pencil at hand to mark boxes, jot ideas that come to mind and might interrupt you - like forgotten phone calls and things for the grocery list. Write down any negative self-talk so you can de-clutter it later on.
- Your timer.
- Some lively music.

4. NO "TRAVELING"

"Traveling" is going from room to room, having projects started in many areas, but none of them finished. For example, when you de-clutter the kitchen utensil drawer, you find an item that belongs in the dining room buffet, so you take it there. Since the buffet is full and a mess, you start to clean out the buffet to make room for the item. You have two rooms in chaos, nothing completed and you run out of time. Aargh!

Stay at the initial project site until you finish. Set aside near the room entranceway any item that doesn't belong at that location. When you finish the project you had planned, take the don't-belong-here item to its proper location. If there is no room for the item there, that location becomes your next project.

PROJECT PROCESS Example: The Sock Drawer

Empty the sock drawer on your bed so you'll finish – or sleep with your socks.
Time allotted: 10 minutes. Set your timer.

THE PROCESS

Step 1. *Ask yourself: Do I wear this pair? YES!*

Sort the socks. Select the socks you wear and return them to the drawer. The socks
you wear are not clutter. Socks left on the bed are socks you do not wear.

Step 2. *Ask yourself: Which of the socks on the bed are Easy (damaged) socks?* – have
holes in them, the elastic is stretched out. They are trash! Put
them in the trash bag.

Question: Are single socks "easy socks?"

A. Example 1: "No! I might find the mate someday."

Produce the evidence: (remember Chapter 17?)
• "What has been my experience? Have I found mates?"
• If you have not found mates, they are easy socks. Toss them out.
• If you have found mates, ask: So what? "Would I wear them if I found the mate?"
• If no, toss the single sock now and if you find the mate, toss that one, too.
• If yes, it is not an easy sock. Keep it. Put it in the drawer.

B. Example 2: "No! Single socks are good for rags!"

Produce the evidence:
What has been my experience? "Do I use socks for rags or do I use paper towels?"
If you use paper towels, single socks are easy socks! Toss them out.
If you use socks for rags, ask:
"How many single socks are a reasonable number of rags?"
Set a limit. Example: use one plastic bag for rags. When the bag is full, don't save
single socks until you use up 1/2 of the bag.

Where are you now? Socks you wear are in the drawer. Damaged socks are in the trash.
Single socks are either in the trash or in the drawer. No more socks on the bed? Put the
drawer back, you are done. Socks on the bed? Read on.

Step 3. *Ask yourself: Am I willing to give the socks on the bed away?*

The socks on the bed are wearable but you don't wear them. They may be the wrong style, for a sport you no longer play or too thick for your shoes, etc. Someone could wear them if you let them go. Put the socks you are willing to give away in a give-away bag.

Can't give all the pairs away? Any socks leftover? What do you do with them?

The miracle is the more we share, the more we have.

Leonard Nimoy

Step 4. Left over socks? Keep Them! Put them in the drawer.
Put the drawer away. Move on to another project.
This is de-clutter, **de-stress** process. Give yourself a break.
(Isn't it great not to have to be perfect!) Keep them. When in doubt, keep it.

Review: Empty a container. Put the items in a pile. Ask yourself:
First: Do I wear (use) them? If yes, keep them. Put them back in the container.
Second: I don't wear (use) them. They are damaged. Trash them.
Third: I don't wear (use) them, but they are wearable (useable). Give them away.
Fourth: I don't wear (use) them. I don't want to let them go. They are leftovers.
Keep them. Put the container back where it belongs. Move on to another project.

Consider the postage stamp;
its usefulness consists of its ability to stick to one thing
until it gets there.

Josh Billings

ADVANTAGES OF A "WHEN IN DOUBT, KEEP IT" PROCESS

* It acknowledges the long-term nature of de-cluttering. You will de-clutter your possessions more than once. The value is in the practice.

* By reducing the fear of making mistakes, it makes you willing to de-clutter more.

* It allows you to not get stuck on one small phase of a larger de-clutter goal. After socks, belts are waiting, so are scarves, etc. Get through socks and move on.

* By allowing you to be kind to yourself, it minimizes regrets so you don't stop.

* It allows you to go through the process with some speed so you don't waste time over the items you are not ready to make decisions about. There is a time and place for everything under heaven. Rather than toss items and regret it, keep them. Move on.

* The anxiety you feel about letting items go is a cue or signal that you have a reason to hold on for a little while longer. You are not ready to let it go. That's okay.

* One phenomena? After you sleep on your decision to keep some leftover items, you may wake up the next morning and decide to let them go.

* When you do decide to let something go, it goes completely -- physically, mentally and emotionally – the first time.

Even the best will in the world, when forced,
achieves nothing.
The best righteousness, when forced,
achieves nothing.
The best good, when forced,
does not come out right . . .

Lao-tzu

GET THE 'NOs' OUT OF THE HOUSE

Put the trash in the trash.
Put the give-aways in your car.
Don't know where to donate your giveaways?

STRATEGY: TELL EVERYONE YOU HAVE THINGS TO DONATE

✳ Go to www.beyondclutter.com/PassItOn for a list of non-profit groups' wish lists.

✳ Ask your pastor, priest or rabbi about any needs that you might be able to fill;

✳ Check your local paper under "garage sales" for ads of organizations having a rummage sale and want donations;

✳ Ask friends, co-workers or neighbors if they know of an organization wanting things;

✳ Ask strangers while waiting in a line or at a church supper.

I see one-third of a nation ill-hosed, ill-clad, ill-nourished…
The test of our progress is not whether we add more
to the abundance of those who have much; it is whether
we provide enough for those who have too little.

Franklin D. Roosevelt

"…then I had a flood in my basement and lost about a third of my books to water damage. I was actually happy to have gotten rid of them, and I realized that if I needed any of them there was always a library. Use the natural disaster criterion to decide what to get rid of. If my books were destroyed by a natural disaster, which ones would I replace? If you wouldn't replace it, then get rid of it."

Dr. Gary S. Aumiller
Keeping It Simple, ©1995, pg. 26

MY EXPERIENCE WITH THE "TELL EVERYONE" STRATEGY

When my Mom died, I chose her bedroom furniture for my guest room which had wall to wall bookcases. I needed to empty the room.

I had emptied a large storage closet at the top of the stairs. I hired a contractor to build library shelving in that closet. That space became the limit on how many books I would keep. I chose my favorites for my new library space.

I practiced my "tell everyone" strategy to find homes for the bookcases. A co-worker's daughter wanted them. When they came for the bookcases, they helped me pack into boxes the 250 books I didn't want into boxes.

Next, I practiced my "tell everyone" strategy to find an organization that could take all the books. At a church supper one night, I asked a woman sitting across the table from me if she knew of any organization that could use 250 books. She named a nursing home in a neighboring town.

When I called the nursing home the next day, the activities director told me she had always wanted to start a library, but her budget was the first one reduced each year so she never had the money. Now she would have the library she always wanted using my books.

The ride to the nursing home was a memorable one. Loading my car became an "event." After I filled the trunk, passenger seat and back seat, there still were boxes of books on the sidewalk. I got in my car and my neighbors unpacked the boxes that were on the sidewalk so they could slide books in here and there. We got them all in my car for the trip to the nursing home. I even had books on my lap. What an adventure!

At the nursing home, the activities director came out to greet me. I sat in the car as employees came and went with books. It was a parade of happiness. Once again, I witnessed clutter converted to joy!

Our days are like identical suitcases – all the same size –
but some people can pack more into them than others.

E-mail gem
author unknown

PROCESS SUMMARY

1. CHOOSE A CATEGORY OR AREA

✽ Start small. Small is a project you can finish in one session.

2. DEDICATE YOUR TIME

✽ Put your commitment on your calendar. Set a timer.

3. BE PREPARED

✽ With a trash and/or recycle bag, a beverage, a pad and pencil and lively music.

4. PROCESS

✽ Put similar items in a pile. Ask:
  First: *Do I use them? Keep.*
  Second: *Are they damaged? Trash.*
  Third: *Am I willing to give them away? Give away bag.*
  Fourth: Leftovers. I don't want to let them go yet. Keep.

5. GET THE 'NOS' OUT OF THE HOUSE

✽ Put the trash in the trash. Put the give aways in your car.

REPEAT

Action may not always bring happiness;
but there is no happiness without action.

Benjamin Disraeli

EXAMPLE OF A DE-CLUTTER GOAL AND PROCESS

GOAL: De-Clutter Your Kitchen

A. Easy Stuff Process (Chapter 11)

Go quickly through the entire kitchen. Look for Easy Stuff (damaged or out-of-date items) to toss out/recycle.

B. Project Process (Chapter 18)

Choose a category. Start with utensils.

Empty the utensil drawer and any utensil holders into a pile on the kitchen counter.

1. Keep: Utensils you use. Put them back into the drawer or holder. All utensils remaining on the counter clutter your life because you do not use them.

2. Toss: Easy Utensils. You don't use these because they are damaged. These are trash.

3. Give Away: Utensils which are still useable and you are willing to let go. Put them in a give away bag.

4. Leftovers: Utensils are still useable, but you are not willing to let them go yet. Keep them. Put them back in the utensil drawer or holder.

5. All utensils are off the counter. Close the drawer. Put back the holder.

6. Choose another small kitchen project by category, such as: dishes, glassware, bake ware, silverware; spices, cereals, canned goods, etc.

Be strong and of good courage.
Do not be afraid or dismayed.

1 Chronicles 22:13

ACCOMPLISHMENT RECORD

Track Your Project Process. Use this page to list one or two goals, small projects you've chosen and start/end dates.

Goals and Projects:	Start or End Date:

Goals and Projects: **Start or End Date:**

CHAPTER 19

Preventive Maintenance

*That which we are, we are
and if we are ever to be any better,
now is the time to begin.*

Alfred Lord Tennyson

PREVENTIVE MAINTENANCE

Just as there is both preventive and corrective medicine, there is preventive and corrective de-cluttering. You have been actively involved in corrective de-cluttering, letting go of clutter you already own. We now turn to preventive strategies. We start with strategies to prevent items you use from becoming clutter.

These strategies are similar to strategies for maintaining a healthy weight or maintaining a weight loss. Food is necessary and food is everywhere. We must learn to manage ourselves around food, make wise food choices, balance in-take and burn-off, since eating and exercising go hand-in-hand. Vigilance and discipline are key.

We also must learn to manage ourselves around things. Things are everywhere. We must own some things. We must learn to manage ourselves around things, to choose carefully the items we bring in and create a regular exercise program of de-cluttering to balance in-take and out-go. If we take in more things than we get rid of, we increase our clutter. Acquiring and letting go, go hand-in-hand. Vigilance and discipline are key.

Preventive maintenance requires you perform "keep-up" daily tasks to manage possessions you use. The objective is to keep your possessions contained within your physical space and time space, so that you live each day fully and not fall behind. That is you are able to start Tuesday on Tuesday rather than start Tuesday by cleaning up Monday.

Well-practiced preventive maintenance strategies reduce the need to set aside time for major de-clutter projects.

Desire is a treasure map.
Knowledge is the treasure chest.
Wisdom is the jewel.
But, without action
they all stay buried.

E-mail gem
author unknown

PREVENTIVE MAINTENANCE STRATEGIES

I. Daily Maintenance

Daily maintenance means putting items you used that day back where they belong - a place for everything *and everything in its place*. Each evening before you go to bed, spend 15 minutes quickly going through the house to put items where they belong. It's a practice that brings closure to your day. Think of this strategy as closing parentheses. We use two parentheses at a time – one to open and one to close. You've opened a day; you close it. Put your house to bed.

How? Start at one end of the house. Work your way room by room. For example, in the living room find the remotes, put them where they belong, put pillows back on the couch, fold up any afghans, put the television guide back where it belongs, straighten up the magazines on the coffee table, etc. Then go to the next room. Work for 15 minutes minimum.

Don't live alone? Rotate or share this responsibility in your living spaces. Rotating the responsibility keeps everyone in line. Sam doesn't get too messy on Tuesday because he knows he has to pick up on Friday. If he creates a huge mess on Tuesday and Tuesday is Mary's day to pick up, on Friday Mary will make a mess for Sam to pick up. The family members police themselves.

If you have more than 15 minutes of daily maintenance, share the responsibility. Everyone pitches in every evening until you get the amount of time down to 15 minutes. Then rotate the responsibility.

Practice. The more you perform daily maintenance tasks the quicker it goes, so you spend less time. To minimize evening pick-up, encourage all family members to pick up after themselves *as they go along*. You'll leave less for the end of the day.

Think 15 minutes doesn't count and you can skip this? Do the Math *(page 35)*.

You're either part of the solution or part of the problem.

Eldridge Cleaver

2. Set Time and/or Space Limits.

By setting a time or space limitation, you decide when a specific preventive maintenance task must be done. Choose whichever type of limit would work best for you.

For example, if you want to prevent a build-up of magazine clutter, you set a :

Time Limitation: *when* a new magazine comes in the mail, you toss or recycle the oldest one of that type.

Space Limitation: Create a magazine basket. *When* the basket becomes full, toss or recycle magazines until the basket is half-empty.

Examples of time or space limits:

- Every garbage night, you find one additional item to throw out.

- If you haven't read unsolicited mail by garbage night, you throw it/them out.

- You wash only clothes that are in the hamper.

- You own only as many books as fit on your bookcases.

- When you buy a book, you select a book to give away/donate.

- When you crack the lid to a plastic container, you throw out both the lid and the container.

History does not long entrust the care of freedom to the weak or the timid. We must acquire proficiency in defense and display stamina in purpose.

Dwight D. Eisenhower

3. Establish Rules of the House

The people who pay the mortgage have the responsibility to set rules of the house which apply to family and visitors alike. Without rules of the house, people think it's okay to put stuff any where, any time and no one seems to have the responsibility to pick things up except mom!

All organizations have rules. The family organization is no different. It's never too late to set them and insist on compliance. Have a family meeting and set the rules – today!

Examples:

- Last person out of a room turns off the lights and any other electronics (TV, DVD, CD player, etc) and puts back all media and the remotes.

- Set four family clean-up times each year when everyone pitches in *for the family as a unit*. For example, at spring, prepare the patio for spring and summer use: hose it down, bring out lawn furniture, wash windows, plant flowers, etc.

- Set minimum standards for children's rooms. Example: set a weekly or monthly inspection. List three to five conditions you will expect. If the room passes your inspection, you will not clean it. If it doesn't, you will clean it and charge them a task as a consequence – they wash the dishes for the next week – or some other exchange.

- Establish a rotating schedule for everyday tasks, such as taking out the garbage, daily evening pick-up, sorting the mail, meal clean-up.

- Assign the behavior that goes with the responsibility, such as "put dirty clothes in the hamper – without being asked twice."

If you do the things you need to do
when you need to do them,
then someday you can do the things
you want to do
when you want to do them.

E-mail: author unknown

"My Dear Children,

As long as you live in this house, you will follow the rules. When you have your own home, then you can make your own rules. In this house we do not have a democracy. You did not vote for me. I didn't campaign to be your father. We are father and children by the grace of God, and therefore, I accept that great privilege and awesome responsibility.

In accepting it, I am going to perform the role of father. Not as a friend or pal; Our ages are too different; I can't play with you as a pal. We can share many things eventually, but we are not just friends. I am much more than a friend — twenty times, a hundred times what a friend is. I'm your father, which includes being a friend, but on a level that is entirely different.

Therefore, we will do in this house as I say. If you know my intent is dictated by love — and that you cannot question because I do love you more than my own life — then my decision will not be easy to take, but easier. So know that I love you, and know that my intent is unquestionable."

Ricardo Montalban
as quoted in *The Mustard Seed*

4. Use it or Lose It

When you find an item you are not using, ask yourself:

When was the last time I used this item? Under what circumstances?
Why aren't I using it?
What is the worst thing that will happen if I let it go?
Is it an irritant?
Is it a distraction?
Could someone else use it now?
Can I borrow it from someone else if I only use it once a year?
Don't use it? Lose it!

If you think you can do a thing or think you can't do a thing, you're right.

Henry Ford

READER'S PREVENTIVE MAINTENANCE PLAN

I. Daily Maintenance. Reader, describe your daily pick up routine:

_____

_____

_____

_____

_____

_____

2. List one time and one space limits here:

I. Time_____

2. Space: _____

3. List two rules of the house you've established.

I. _____

2. _____

Preventive Maintenance Summary:

1. Daily Maintenance
2. Time and Space Limits
3. Rules of the House
4. Use It or Lose It!

There is just one way to bring up a child
in the way he should go
and that is to travel that way yourself.

Abraham Lincoln

CHAPTER 20

Preventive Strategies

If we are always arriving and departing,
it is also true that we are eternally anchored.
One's destination is never a place,
but rather a new way of looking at things.

Henry Miller

PREVENT "POTENTIAL" CLUTTER
Making acquisition conscious

You can compromise your de-clutter efforts by continuing your excess buying habits. You need strategies to help you not buy things which would clutter your life. The more you practice not-buying strategies, the easier they become. You learn to make wise possession choices. This discernment comes with practice.

PREVENTION STRATEGIES

1. Front Door Rule of Life

Live Intelligently. To avoid tempting ourselves with certain foods, we don't bring them home through the front door. Apply that strategy to possessions. If you think you want an item, use the front door strategy to help you change your mind by thinking of the true price of owning it.

Remind yourself that if you don't bring the item in the front door, you'll have no responsibility for it. No decisions to make. No time or energy to be spent caring for it.

Ask yourself these questions:
- Could I look at it every day?
- Do I have room for it?
- Do I know where it is going to go?
- Do I want to dust it every week?
- Does it need special cleaning supplies, treatment?
- Dry clean only? "hand-wash cold"? wash/clean separately?
- Will it wrinkle easily? (that means the dreaded iron!)

Other implications:

- Will it draw the family together or make it stronger? Or
- Will it cause discord either in terms of use or cost?
- Have you gotten tired or bored by your last purchase?
- Are you willing to sacrifice the time, money and energy it might require?

Okay, Helen, I'm to make decisions to purchase things with full awareness of the cost in time, money and energy of possessing it. What else can I do to resist the urge to buy?

2. Help Yourself Wait!

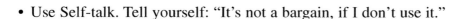

Examples:

Live Patiently. Don't shop the day you see a sales flyer with an item you think you want. Wait.

If you feel an urge...

- Use Self-talk. Tell yourself: "It's not a bargain, if I don't use it."

- Let Fate Step In. Decide that if you are meant to have the item, it will be there.

- Cool Off. Give yourself a five-day "cooling off" period. Delay may quell the impulse. If you still feel the compulsion five days later, go ahead.

- Don't Drop Everything. Refuse to allow the quest of a material object to interrupt your life.

- Have Faith: This, too, will pass! The feeling that you have to have it now will pass. There will be another sale.

- Create Substitutes for Shopping. Shopping maybe a habit. Replace buying trips with other activities. Make a list of activities you could do instead of shopping so when you feel the urge to shop, you'll have something else to do with your time.

Ask yourself:

✳ Do I need it?
✳ Is it worth my time and effort to get in the car, drive, park, walk, wait in line, purchase, walk, drive home and park again?
✳ What's the best use of my time?
✳ Am I willing to die for it? (Most accidents happen within five miles of home.)

Okay, Helen, if after I tell myself to wait, I still want it, what's next?

I want to think about it.

Rev. Dr. Martin Luther King Jr.
(his standard response when asked to make a snap decision)

3. Pay As You Go

Live Frugally. Become less willing to go into debt for possessions. Keep bill paying, financial paper management and the income you use to support debt, as simple as possible.

Many of our parents' and our grandparents' generations lived by a rule when it came to money: if they didn't have the cash on hand, they didn't buy anything. Since debt is a major cause of stress today, consider this preventive strategy carefully.

- Reduce your credit cards. Eliminate those for only one store.

- Pay with cash, by check or debit card.

- Use credit cards only for major or emergency purchases or purchases that can only be done with a credit card, like airplane, hotel or rental car reservations.

- Tell yourself: No money? No buy.

Okay, Helen, I get the idea. So what if I do buy an item?

4. The Front Door Rule Responsibility Corollary

Live Responsibly. If you bring an item through the front door be responsible for it. What is being a "responsible" owner? In my opinion, responsibility is knowing where all of your things are and keeping every thing in good working condition.

If one of your possessions breaks or otherwise needs repair, you are presented with a choice. The broken, non-working item is clutter. You can restore it to good working condition or toss it. Making the choice timely is a responsibility of ownership.

Okay, Helen, what if I bring the item in the front door? What then?

5. Practice: One In – One Out

Live Consciously. Clutter control is analogous to breathing. We inhale then exhale, one right after the other. It's automatic. One in, one out. We inhale and exhale in equal proportion. We don't inhale on even days and exhale on odd days. If we hold our breath, the next thing we do is exhale – that is, let go.

Practice the same strategy with possessions. When you acquire an item, let go of an item. De-cluttering is the second half of the acquiring process, the exhale. Inhale, exhale; acquire, let go, one right after the other. With practice, letting go becomes automatic.

This practice will maintain your possession level. You will not own **more**.

When do you let go? *Immediately* after you acquire.
(Do you wait to exhale? No!)

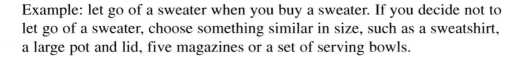

Okay Helen, what do I let go of?

Same Size Criteria

Let go of an item (or a combination of items) of similar size to the one you acquire.

Example: let go of a sweater when you buy a sweater. If you decide not to let go of a sweater, choose something similar in size, such as a sweatshirt, a large pot and lid, five magazines or a set of serving bowls.

If you buy an item in a box, fill the box with items you will let go of.

Keep the box? Let go of a box or a same size item for that, too.

Helen, what do I keep?

I am only one. But still, I am one.
I cannot do everything, but still, I can do something.
And because I cannot do everything, I will not refuse to do the something that I can do.

Edward Everett Hale

6. Standard for Ownership: Use or Joy

Live Practically. Keep items you use. So long as you use it, an item isn't clutter.

Live Joyfully. Celebrate the emotional side of your personality. Think of it as "joy." Some items remind us of special times, places and people in our lives.

Other people say to keep items you "love." Leo Buscaglia said one shouldn't love something that can't love them back. I changed my thinking and changed my standard to joy!

What do you own? Items that you use plus items that bring you joy.

When you stop using an item or when an item stops bringing you joy, the item becomes clutter and it's time to let go of it.

Okay, Helen, how many items do I keep? How do I know when enough is enough?

7. The Standard of Reasonableness

Live Reasonably. Keep a reasonable number of items that you use, plus a reasonable number of items that bring you joy. Keep them for a reasonable length of time.

Reasonable depends on your use. For measuring cups, three or four would be reasonable for most of us. For someone who bakes regularly six or seven may be reasonable.

Reasonableness is directly related to space limitations. The Shakers taught us: a place for everything, and everything in its place. When you run out of space or find yourself jamming things into drawers, you are exceeding what is reasonable for the space. Filling space is one of the first early warning signals that we are beginning to clutter again.

Okay, Helen. Early warning signals? What are they?

It is the pre-occupation with possession more than anything else,
that prevents man from living freely and nobly.

Bertrand Russell

8. Early Warning Signals

Live Attentively. Develop indicators to warn that you are acquiring "more." These signs spark action to de-clutter. Pay attention to:

- Are you filling a space that had been empty?

- Is a table top, dresser top, counter top, or windowsill filling up?

- Are you shoving things into drawers?

- Does each room still look uncluttered?

- Do you feel calm, relaxed, at peace in your house?

- Have you looked for an item that was not where it belonged?

- Are you still telling others about your de-cluttering successes?

Still the question recurs "can we do better?'
The dogmas of the quiet past are inadequate
to the stormy present. The occasion is piled
high with difficulty, and we must rise with the occasion.
As our case is new, so we must think anew,
and act anew.

Abraham Lincoln

MY EXPERIENCE: I ATTEND GARAGE SALES

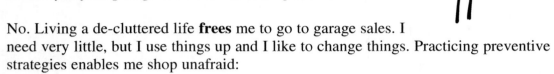

"Isn't that contrary to living a de-cluttered life?"
"Aren't you afraid you won't be able to resist a bargain?"
"Don't you find garage sales too much temptation?"

No. Living a de-cluttered life **frees** me to go to garage sales. I
need very little, but I use things up and I like to change things. Practicing preventive
strategies enables me shop unafraid:

• I buy to replace. If I get an item, I purge an item. One in, one out!

• I don't buy just because an item is a "bargain." It's not a bargain if I don't use it.

• While I decide whether to buy an item, I carry it around for a while. Sometimes just
holding it is enough. I put it back when I leave.

• Check out line? If there's a line to check out, I re-think my purchase, weighing it
against moving on to the next garage sale. Often, I decide the item is not worth
waiting for.

• I enjoy the experience of "garaging." I go with a friend, talk with nice people, see all
kinds of things and drive through neighborhoods I didn't know existed.

• I often see things my family had when I was growing up so I have the chance to
reminisce. I peruse as if I were in a museum – I take my time to look and accept that
the items will stay there – just as if it were a museum.

• What do I look for?
    I buy things I use up: candles, wrapping paper, office supplies, jig saw puzzles,
    soaps, lotions, towels, etc.
    I buy things to give away, such as organizing tools for clients.

• Seeing what things are priced at garage sales reminds me how de-valued most of our
possessions become. That motivates me not to acquire in the first place.

Make up your mind to be happy. Learn to find pleasure in simple things.

Robert Louis Stevenson

PREVENTION STRATEGIES SUMMARY

I. Front Door Rule of Life
- Live Intelligently. Don't bring it in the front door.

2. Help Yourself Wait
- Live Patiently. Delay purchasing.

3. Pay As You Go
- Live Frugally. No money, no buy.

4. The Front Door Rule Responsibility Corollary
- Live Responsibly. Keep your possessions in good working order.

5. Practice: One In/One Out
- Live Consciously. When you acquire, let go.
- Same Size Criteria
    Let go of items of the same size

6. Standard for Ownership: Use or Joy
- Live Practically. Live joyfully. Keep only items you use or bring you joy.

7. The Standard of Reasonableness
- Live Reasonably. Own a reasonable number of things, for a reasonable time.

8. Early Warning Signals
- Live Attentively. Develop visual cues to prevent re-cluttering your life.

It wasn't raining when Noah built the ark.

Howard Ruff
The 2,548 Best Things Anybody Ever Said

CHAPTER 21

Gift Giving and Gift Receiving Policy

———⊷◦⊶———

If my hands are fully occupied in holding on to something,
I can neither give nor receive.

Dorothee Solle

———⊷◦⊶———

INTRODUCTION

Gift giving and receiving is a time when we invite others into our dance with possessions. Refuse to give or receive clutter disguised as a gift.

Do you have difficulty letting go of things given to you by someone else? Gifts add an emotional component to an otherwise simple answer to the question, "Is it clutter?" The gift has no use, but the person may be special, the event may be special or, heaven forbid, the giver may ask to see their "gift" when they come to visit. You feel obligated to keep the gift, because it was a "gift." If it wasn't a gift, if you bought it for yourself, it would have been long gone!

Being on a clutter-free path affords you an opportunity to change your gifting rules: you become clear on what you will accept as gifts, become more willing to tell others what you want and ask others what they want.

If you think that gift giving has gotten out of hand, chances are others in your circle do, too. They may be grateful that you brought the matter up. It takes one courageous person to do so. That is a gift in itself.

When you bring an uncluttered consciousness to gifting, you reduce the stress of the process and return it to a joy-filled activity — for everyone. That's a gift in itself.

Take three steps:
* Examine your gift-giving and gift-receiving habits.
* Set gift-giving and gift-receiving policies.
* Tell others what *your* policies are; ask others what their policies are.

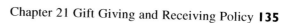

You accomplish:
* In your choice of a gift to give someone else, you set a tone and model a style of giving that is clutter-free and less stress-filled,
* You prevent others from giving you clutter – things you will not use, not bring you joy or not otherwise fit in your de-cluttered way of living, and
* You affirm the value of the relationship as a higher value by putting people before things.

We are the choices we make.

Meryl Streep

PREPARATION: TELL EVERYONE STRATEGY

Don't wait until the gift giving/receiving event is near. Start now to chat with friends and family about your change to a de-cluttered lifestyle. Make "general announcements" at family get togethers, parties and in casual conversation so everyone knows about your new de-cluttered style of living. In the announcements, get around to the topic of gifts.

Include some or all of the following:

- Announce "I have decided to de-clutter my life."
- Give one or two ways clutter made your life more stressful.
- Explain how good it feels that you can find things and other benefits.
- Mention your new standard of owning things – use or bring joy.
- Exclaim that you'd be happy never to see a (name a type of item) again.
- Invite other people to support you.
- Conclude with a specific statement about gifts, such as:
    "From now on, I only want gifts that get used up, such as..." or
    "I only want things I can use, such as..."

Effect?

- As you inform everyone of your experience, you set the stage for change.
- You indirectly tell them what gifts you don't want.
- You spare people's feelings by not singling out any one person for their past gifts.
- Alert everyone you may ask to change rules about gifts.

Timing

Because people have a variety of gift buying habits and you are asking them to change, be sensitive to the timing of your request. You have been thinking about a change, they haven't. The idea is new to them. Give enough time for them to consider your request.

The worst time to bring up a change in gift giving for Christmas is a few weeks before Christmas. For most people that is too late. This Christmas, you could talk about change for next Christmas or talk about your April birthday wishes.

Our lives begin to end the day we become silent about things that matter.

Rev. Dr. Martin Luther King, Jr.

GIFT GIVING AND RECEIVING POLICIES

Consider this example of a very simple policy:

"On holidays, gifts must be for the family.
Individuals may receive gifts on their birthday."

Talk to people with whom you exchange gifts to brainstorm changes in gifting rules.

• Agree not to trade meaningless items.

• Agree to only exchange cards this year.

• Meet friends for an event, such as lunch and a movie or museum. Agree the time spent together is your gift to each other, rather than a "thing."

• Give and receive gifts which will be used up so that no "thing" remains. Examples:

> Certificates for: dinner out, car wash, house cleaning, a massage, day at a spa, a free lesson in the hobby of choice, a hot air balloon ride, a load of firewood.

> gifts of service: rake leaves, take an older or disabled friend shopping; baby sit for harried parents;

> Create a stationary package with letterhead or note cards, postage stamps, address labels, "Thank You" cards.

> A catalog from a local community college plus tuition for a course of choice.

• Agree to jointly give large, expensive gifts.

• Throw a party. Everyone brings a gift of food to share! The time together and food are the gifts to each other.

Never doubt that a small group of thoughtful,
committed citizens can change the world;
indeed, it's the only thing that ever has.

Margaret Mead

READER'S EXERCISE: Prepare to change gifting rules.

List one or two events where you could make your general announcement.

1. _____

2. _____

List four people who may be willing to talk with you about changing gift policies.

1. _____ 3. _____

2. _____ 4. _____

Jot down notes for your announcement.

One way clutter made your life more stressful. _____

Name a specific item or type of item you let go of _____

Benefits of de-cluttering your life _____

Name items you do not want _____

Name items you would like _____

Law number ten: Stuff doesn't make you happy; you do.
I think this law speaks for itself.
You know the drill: Money can't buy happiness.
Well, it's the same with stuff.
Both are just tools to help you achieve your own happiness.

Georgene Lockwood
The Complete Idiot's Guide to Organizing Your Life © 1999

 **CONGRATULATIONS!**

When you feel like you might back slide into yo-yo cluttering,
RUN - don't walk - to this book, turn to this page and read:

DO YOU LIVE YOUR DASH!

I read of a man who stood to speak
At the funeral of a friend
He referred to the dates on her tombstone
From the beginning… to the end.

He noted that first came her date of birth
And spoke the following date with tears,
But he said what mattered most of all
Was the dash between those years.
(1934 - 1998)

For that dash represents all the time
That she spent alive on earth…
And now only those who loved her
Know what that little line is worth.

For it matters not, how much we own;
The cars… the house… the cash,
What matters is how we live and love
 And how we spend our dash.

So think about this long and hard…
Are there things you'd like to change?
For you never know how much time is
left, That can still be rearranged.

If we could just slow down enough
To consider what's true and real,
And always try to understand
The way other people feel.

And be less quick to anger,
And show appreciation more
And love the people in our lives
Like we've never loved before.

If we treat each other with respect,
And more often wear a smile…
Remembering that this special dash
Might only last a little while.

So, when your eulogy's being read
With your life's actions to rehash…
Would you be proud of the things they say
About how you spent your dash?

Author Unknown

INDEX OF MOTIVATIONAL QUOTATIONS

To Hire Helen

For information on workshops, talks and
downsizing services
offered by the author, see her web site:
www.beyondclutter.com

Comments and Experiences with this book

*To share your experiences with this book,
address them to the author at:*

Beyond Clutter
100 White Pine Drive #413
Albany, NY 12203-6403

or by E-mail to
helen@beyondclutter.com

About the Author

Helen Volk, B.S., J.D., is the Founder and President of Beyond Clutter, a firm that helps people de-clutter, de-stress their lives. Beyond Clutter is a New York State Certified Woman-Owned Business.

She conducts sessions for corporations, businesses and individuals on the attitudes, habits and skills needed to organize one's self, work and life. Ms. Volk is an Elderhostel instructor (Pack Rats Can Change!), created the continuing legal education class, "The Organized Attorney," and leads a de-clutter support group.

As an expert in her field, Helen is an accomplished motivational speaker who speaks regularly to professional groups and conferences. Albany's first professional organizer, she has been featured in all local newspapers and is sought out by broadcast and print media for information on de-cluttering one's life.

A certified experienced teacher and lawyer who practiced law for 17 years before creating Beyond Clutter in 1991, Ms. Volk was a pack rat who chose to simplify her life in the early-80's and live clutter-free. Her decision to change her style of living and her story of transition serve as inspiration to her students and clients.

Helen Volk is a Golden Circle member of the National Association of Professional Organizers (NAPO), and founding member of the Capital Area Professional Organizers. She is a graduate of the Dale Carnegie Course, Literacy Volunteer and Community Mediation training.

Helen is a recipient of the "Woman of Excellence" Award for Excellence in Business from the Women's Business Council of the Albany-Colonie Regional Chamber of Commerce. She was profiled in SUNY Alumni in Business and Industry, honoring selected State University of New York (SUNY) Alumni for their success in business, service to the community and support of education.

She was the first woman chair of the Municipal Law Section of the New York State Bar Association; founded the Capital District Chapter of the Women's Bar Association of the State of New York; president of her condominium board of managers and resident advisory council.